TESTIMONIALS

"The guide to a better life. A whole new world and a better way of thinking. Never mind lipstick in your bag, get a copy of this book, and smile inside and out.

"The guide to become that person you always dreamed of being. It does what it says on the label, no gimmicks just a better life.

"The forecast for the days ahead are bright and full of joy. I can only describe Helen as womankind's answer to Paul McKenna!

"Grab yourself a copy now"

Karen Woods: Author of the best selling novel Broken Youth

"It was such an amazing journey meeting Helen. When I first met her I had been yo-yo dieting on and off for a few years. And had tried all the diets under the sun. I had even tried hypnosis before but nothing seemed to work, then I was recommended to Helen.

"I'm glad I went because it truly changed my life she stayed with me throughout. The difficult first few weeks. I've never experienced anything quite like it before, I really didn't have any urges to eat like I had previously, some of her techniques seem strange but they work and that's truly amazing so...I recommend her to anyone.

Beverley Jones, Client

*

The Female Paul McKenna has arrived

"I believe Helen can cure anyone anytime of many problems and illnesses. People have accused her work as being like Paul McKenna's but I think they are wrong! She's better!! The later parts of the book prove that!

"Get a fab read with so much information on so many different aspects of this subject. Well worth a look - you never know it could just change your life too.

Angela Williamson

*

Magic in Action

"I've known of Helen's unique therapy for ages and I was so terrified about giving birth, with it being my first time, that I immediately called upon her talents to cure my fear of labour.

"I had the most AMAZING hypnotherapy sessions, to the point where her techniques have completely changed my entire life. I now cannot WAIT to embrace the journey into Motherhood.

"Without her help, I really have no idea how I would've coped. There's something truly magical and mysterious as well as motherly about her...with a youthful, honest, northern warmth...

"She has an incredible talent and I'm not surprised she has finally made it and is in such big demand. I'm so happy that the world finally gets to benefit from what I call her 'magic.'"

Chrissie Wunna - Star of 'Paris Hilton's Second Best British Friend "

UNLEASH THE GENIUS WITHIN

Helen Kelly

EMPIRE
PUBLICATIONS

First published in 2011

EMPIRE PUBLICATIONS
1 Newton Street, Manchester M1 1HW
© Helen Kelly 2011

ISBN 1 901 746 75 5 - 9781901746754

Printed in Great Britain.

CONTENTS

	Preface - A Letter from The Author	9
	Thanks	14
	Introduction	15
1	Can I really Change My Life?	21
2	Getting Ready	25
3	Emotions	32
4	Your Inner Critic	41
5	Super Confidence	44
6	Emotional Intelligence	49
7	Positivity and why it's important	54
8	Start creating your own future now	60
9	Your Personal Genie	65
10	Make It Happen	70
11	You Don't Have to be Clever Academically	76
12	Power To Heal	85
13	The Power of Napping	95
14	Little Genie Diet	98
15	The Laughter Effect	117
16	Believe in Yourself	119
17	Your Right to Be Rich	129
18	Clear Your Mind, Prepare to Shine	138
19	The Intelligence of Thinking	144
20	Secret Teachings	148
21	Happy Factor	161
22	The Trouble With Psychology	168
23	The Magic Gland	173
24	Mind and Body Awareness	181
25	The Study of Wealth	191
26	Stay Healthy	197
27	Using Your Own Energy	212
28	Trees and Healing Energy	223
29	Learning Should Be Fun	225

PREFACE

A letter from the author

I was born in Haworth, West Yorkshire the second youngest of nine children. At the age of eleven my sixteen year old brother died after a motorbike accident and my father took his own life the day of his funeral. My mother was left to cope with eight children. Eventually this twist of fate was to cause untold damage to my family who all took different paths in life. I became withdrawn and was singled out in school as a dyslexic who couldn't even write one line and, as a result, my confidence suffered for many years. I chose the wrong partners in life who abused me and deep inside I believed I was a failure who no one would listen to.

As the years passed I had three children to a man who both physically and mentally abused me including cheating on me with several women. My confidence was at an all time low and for a while I felt suicidal. Eventually I ended up having a nervous breakdown. When I came out of hospital something happened that changed my life forever.

It was early evening as I lay on my bed in a three bedroom flat that I still shared with my abusive husband who was a big

London gangster. The sun was just going down as I peered out of the bedroom window and as I closed my eyes, I thought I must have nodded off, when the strangest thing happened. I felt myself ascending out of my own body. It was as if a cord was attached to me from my belly button. This cord kept pulling me out and then as I was coming out of my body, I turned to see myself lying there on the bed. At first I thought I had died and that I was looking back at myself but something kept pushing me back into the body on the bed. No matter how hard I tried something kept pushing me back.

I didn't feel scared at all, in-fact I'd never felt better, as if something was being confirmed to me from the other side.

I eventually realised this was one of the best things that had ever happened to me. I knew that I had to change my life or die, so as I waited for dawn to break the following morning (I knew my husband would be going out to work on one of his many deals in the crime world) I packed a few clothes and took my three children with me and paid for a single ticket to Manchester. I don't know why I chose Manchester – it was as if I was being told that that was where I should go, despite having no connections there.

When I arrived some four hours later I took myself to the nearest hostel for battered women. My husband kept trying to find me as I began to re-build my life. Then I found out he had died of a heart attack as a result of his hard living – his drinking, smoking, womanising and a bad diet. I felt it was still my duty to sort out the funeral and bury the man I had once thought I loved and shared my life with. As I was standing there and his body was lowered into the ground I remember thinking – what a waste of life.

I vowed then to change mine forever.

I enrolled on courses to enable me to learn basic writing and reading skills and as I had always been curious about how the human mind works I decided to enrol on a course in Psychology in order to help me understand myself better. After three years of study and continual learning I had the confidence to stand up for myself.

As a child I never spoke much, mostly because I didn't think anyone cared what I had to say. I would write my thoughts down on paper, in my own way. I loved writing and even though no-one taught me at school, it was as if I had a thirst for learning that I never had when I was at school. I couldn't get enough. It wasn't that I couldn't learn, it was more that I had never been taught.

I eventually married a second time to a professional magician, who was the kindest man I ever met. Little did I know that five years down the line I would be burying my second husband and my life would take another twist.

When Jack died on the 22nd May 2002 to bowel cancer at the age of 44 I decided I would go back to study yet again and further my career. Then one day out of the blue I was engrossed in a programme on television about hypnosis and a curious thing called NLP (Neuro Linguistic Programming). I was mesmerised and wanted to know more so off I went to the local bookshop and found myself wandering through the self-help books where I found a book by Paul McKenna the famous self-help guru.

Although the book advised me to read it in seven days, I

finished it in one. I never could keep my nose out of a good book. In the back of that book I found a telephone number for courses in NLP and Hypnosis.

I decided if I was going to learn this stuff I was going to learn from the best, so I took my first steps into the unknown and enrolled on a course with Paul McKenna and Michael Neill, a celebrity coach to the rich and famous and the co-creator of NLP Dr Richard Bandler.

As I travelled to London I was both excited and frightened at the prospect of meeting these three gurus. My life changed forever that first day, it was as if something deep in my psyche was being confirmed. I will always be grateful to these three great men who set me on this journey of self-discovery.

From there I couldn't get enough. I wanted to know more about myself and the world we live in so I travelled the globe, studying Yoga, Vibrational Medicine, Psychology, the Shoalin Monks, Clinical Hypnosis, Quantum Touch, TFT (Thought Field Therapy) Physics, Macrobiotics and 'Do-In', which is a very ancient Japanese discipline that is virtually unheard of in the west. When I returned to England I continued my research on successful people and what makes them tick.

My findings have been wide and varied but always exciting. I finally put together "Unleash The Genius Within". This book is written for those who wish to learn more about themselves and the amazing planet we live on and to try a fresh approach to life's complexities.

Within these pages you will find answers to most of life's common problems and deeper issues including how to change your life for the better.

Preface

Consider this: What would you do if no one was looking?

Live your life everyday as if no one was looking and watch as your dreams unfold before you.

For my part I am giving you all that I have learned and hope you will benefit from learning something new as I did all those years ago.

THANKS

To Paul McKenna, Richard Bandler and Michael Neill, my clients, colleagues and friends all of whom I could not have written this book without.

To my children Kelly, Maria, Katie Ellen, and Paul Anthony, thank you for supporting me and believing in my dream. And to my husband Rob who has loved me unconditionally and who has given me the greatest joy and happiness for eight years.

And with special thanks to my best friend Karen who has always been dynamic and inspiring throughout writing this book - together we have conquered all our dreams.

Finally, to Angela my friend and companion on our endless walks through the countryside, where my ideas seem to flow effortlessly.

INTRODUCTION

When I first started this book it was just an idea put together from years of research into the human mind and how closely our psychology and physiology work together.

We all know how many self help books are out there and I would encourage you to read them all, I guarantee you will learn something new from all of them – I should know, I've read most of them.

The more knowledge you have, the more power and influence you bring into your life. There is an old cliché that practice makes perfect and it's true.

The techniques you will learn in 'Unleash the Genius Within' are truly amazing. I believe there are only a small handful of people who understand the full universal laws and how to use them in order to make their lives better. But, I'm a great believer in people; I believe people will make the right choices when they know the truth; so my job is to spread the word and hope you will become one of those people.

If this is true, you may ask 'Why isn't everyone rich and successful?' Well, mostly because everyone starts out with good intentions to practice new skills for a while but then they give up. Now I know some of you will be saying 'I've heard that one before' and you probably have but it's still true. Look at Thomas Edison for example – he failed 8000 times before he eventually invented the light bulb and when someone asked him how it felt to have failed 8000 times he replied, "I didn't fail 8000 times, I just found 8000 ways that didn't work".

Now that's the power of positive thought, but that's what make people like Thomas Edison different. Using his mindset you could be one of those naturally positive people.

You have to be prepared for failure in order to succeed – this is a prerequisite to all true success; most people give up after a few attempts.

If you want something badly enough, work at it and don't expect it to happen overnight, but you can start to make it happen overnight, that's the difference.

There is a formula for success and if you follow it you will be guaranteed to succeed. And I don't just mean financial success, I mean success in any area of your life that you feel the need for change.

Sometimes people learn from those who only think they are good but are not, make sure your teacher explains it to you in a way you can understand, I always make sure the person teaching me is one of the best at what he/she does because I have found if you learn from the best you can become the best.

I learned something wonderful from a teacher of mine Dr Richard Bandler, the co-creator of NLP (Neuro Linguistic Programming) who said people are not stuck they just need to re-program their minds.

Let's face it, if you are relying on an old desktop computer you would need to update the software in order to be able to do the things you need from it today, as computers just keep evolving.

Well it's the same with our brains. Only we never sit and think that our brains need updating. That's when we become stuck. Your brain is the most advanced bio computer in the world, so it doesn't make sense not to update it. An upgrade is long overdue in my opinion. When I reviewed all the old programmes I was running in my brain, I never saw such success in my life.

Now for me it was a big deal. I needed to learn, and I wanted to learn from the best, so in order to do that I researched into the human potential field and found numerous ways from psychology to hypnosis to NLP to old Chinese monks and I studied and learned from them all.

'Unleash The Genius Within' comes from years of study and learning what works in all of these areas and combining them to produce a truly magical and powerful example of an almost perfect human being.

I will share with you amazing techniques not only to help rid yourself of negativity and create more positive feelings, but I will teach you how you can have an abundance of health and well-being and tap into the secrets of longevity.

Don't just put up with what you have, you can do more and create happiness, health and amazing wealth when you open your mind to these new techniques and put them into practice.

Believe in yourself and watch as your dreams unfold before you. Learn the secrets to true and lasting success in every area of your life.

You have more power than you could ever imagine.

When was the last time you did something different? Be bold and start it today and look forward to your success.

Indeed you can start right now.

If you're reading this as you lie in bed, why not try reading it at a time of day you wouldn't normally read? We do things habitually every day of our lives and whilst there isn't anything wrong with that, we could potentially be missing out on other things, so why not try something different?

I know a man who came to me for help who said "but I can't change, I won't know myself". I asked him to try changing something really simple at the beginning of each day, you know what he did – he started wearing his watch on his left wrist instead of his right. You may want to be bolder and wear a blue sock on one foot and a red sock on the other or even wear something totally out of character, it's entirely up to you but that simple change made him constantly aware he could change anything in his life at any time. This empowered him to slowly change the things in his life which he wasn't happy with and to know he was in control of his own destiny.

You could start today.

Maybe you could take a different route to work – do you always take the same road to get there? Well try a different route, you may not get there any quicker but you will see different things and your experience will be totally different.

Throughout this book I want you to experience some

change in your everyday life. If you're totally committed it will come easily, if you're not maybe you're just not the kind of person who wants to try new things. It's not that you can't, everyone can change anything anytime, it's more you are resisting change, so maybe you should explore your fears of change first and see if there is some irrational fear holding you back from being the best you can be.

At the end of the day it's all up to you; remember though, if you're not entirely happy with what you have in your life right now, you have the power within to change it. What would you do if your life depended on it? Take this mindset and use it to your advantage in every area of your life.

A great friend of mine once said "What would you do if no one was looking?" Live your life as if no one is looking and see how good your life can be.

The Power of the Mind

Your mind is the most advanced bio-computer in the world, some people think that desk tops and laptops are really clever machines (and they are) but who invented them? We did of course and computers are nowhere near as clever and smart as we are, so next time you look at one remember it doesn't have anywhere near your mind's capacity for learning. We use less than half our brain power and yet we do the most amazing things every day, so imagine what more we could do if we used more of it.

When you read through this book it should empower you to explore your own capabilities and to reach heights you previously thought impossible.

Your brain is made up of billions of cells, I know some scientists like to state exact figures, but I prefer to say there are billions; your brain is arguably the most complex machine in the universe. Somehow it generates our own consciousness and determines our thoughts and actions. No human being alive still fully understands our brain and all its complexities. There is another saying that, "If you put rubbish in, you will only get rubbish out". Think about that? Isn't it time to upgrade our brains?

You are born with a unique code. No other human being is the same; you may have similarities but never the same genetic code. Neuroscientists accept they have a huge challenge ahead of understanding the finite capacity of the brain.

Just think – every breath you take, every beat of your heart; every movement and every emotion are controlled directly or indirectly by the nervous system of which the brain is the ultimate part. We know the brain is not just a centre for issuing instructions – it is constantly under attack from internal and external information.

From the moment we are born, we use all of our senses to make sense of the world in which we live. These five senses are smell, taste, sight, sound and touch.

And before we learned how to use our conscious ability we relied on these five senses far more to make sense of the world around us.

1

The book you hold in your hands has the power to change your life forever.

How do I know that?

I've helped hundreds of people just like you achieve their goals and the success they want – often exceeding their own expectations.

Don't think you can do it?

Well you're in for a shock – never underestimate the power of your mind.

"Unleash The Genius Within" is a mind manual full of instructions to change the unhelpful habits you have stored in your subconscious mind. You will discover things you never thought possible and once you start putting them into practice you'll be amazed at the results.

Success is predictable if you're willing to give it a go, so why not get comfortable, sit down and read this book then change your own life for the better.

Enjoy The Ride!

Can I really Change My Life?

In one simple sentence – Yes you can.

People get stuck in a rut not because they want to but because they get caught up in life as it rolls along but when you start to use the techniques in this book you will soon break the old habits that hold you back from achieving your dreams.

Firstly you need to establish the changes you want to make, the things that are important to you. Sit and think of the most important things in your life now and make a list in your mind - what do I really want? Now do the same with all things you don't want – list them in your head or on paper – what don't I want.

If you're like most people you have probably been focusing on the things you don't want in your life instead of the things you do. It's not your fault, we just tend to think the worst because we are afraid that if we think the best it will somehow backfire on us, or we think "well I'm not that lucky". Either way I want you to know you're not alone.

An example of this is people tell themselves: I won't get that job I'm not that lucky, pre-supposing someone else will get it that deserves it more than you. Whether it's a conscious or unconscious decision, you have made an assumption that you're not worthy of the job. Then, when you get the letter or phone call confirming your belief, you feel even worse.

If this sounds familiar then you need to start changing your beliefs because what we focus our attention most on is what we get.

Beliefs are just that – they are neither truths nor lies, so let's start instilling some more positive beliefs in your head. If you start each day making small changes, changes you may not even recognise at first, as each day goes by you will begin to realise just how far you have come.

The techniques in 'Unleash The Genius Within' are up to date, state-of-the-art mind changing software for your brain, it's a bit like a user manual for your brain that we weren't given at birth.

If you do anything consistently for two weeks it will change you. What makes 'Unleash The Genius Within' so different is that it not only helps update your mind's software but it will keep on working throughout your life forever.

The purpose of this book and my system is to help you get control of your brain and have greater control over everything in your life. Just as a car needs a service every 6 months, so does your brain. If it doesn't get a service it will not operate to its full potential and will breakdown and then take some considerable time before it runs properly again.

Similarly if you are still using old software on an old computer you will find that it soon becomes obsolete. Unfortunately, as humans we don't often think of this for ourselves so we end up running on the same old software given to us from birth.

Together we are going to install some up to date software and eliminate the old software to enable you to make those long overdue changes.

We currently live in the most advanced information age. From mobile phones to faxes, desk tops to laptops, these gadgets are now considered normal parts of life when sixty years ago they were probably not even dreamt about.

This is proof as to the power of your mind because everything you see is manmade, so if we are capable of such great things using only a fraction of the brain power available to us can you imagine what we are truly capable of if we were to use more of it and more often.

I believe we are on a threshold of the next great leap in evolution and people will not only want information but we will move into the mind technology age where people will want to understand and use more of their own inner resources, so what seemed impossible sixty years ago is now a reality and so it will be in another sixty years we will continue to evolve at an alarming rate.

You have all that is needed to evolve, grow and learn everyday of your life, your brain is the most advanced bio-computer in the world – so why not get to know it more? Become friends with it and you will experience the most amazing transformation in your life.

2

Getting Ready

Taking control of your life is the first thing you need to do and I mean *you*. You must take full responsibility for what you do from today.

No one likes the word responsibility because today no one seems to want to take responsibility for anything; people pass the buck so things that happen in our lives that go wrong can be blamed on someone or something else.

But another ideal way of thinking about responsibility is control. Do you want to control your life or are you willing to let other people take control of it? Do you want to master your emotions or be a victim for the rest of your life? It's all down to choices we make so what choices will you make today.

Taking control of all the things in your life that you can control and letting go of all the things you can't is your first step to being responsible. It's too easy for people to blame others – government, family or friends but until you make the changes inside your head to take full responsibility for yourself then you don't have the power to change it.

All the most successful people in history know this principle and live their lives accordingly to it.

Einstein explained it like this: "Communities tend to be guided less than individuals by conscience and a sense of responsibility. How much misery does this fact cause mankind! It is the source of wars and every kind of oppression, which fill the earth with pain, sighs and bitterness." (Albert Einstein, 1934)

Beliefs: Discover your true potential

Your first step into making all your wishes come true is the beliefs you have about yourself and the world you live in.

When you are born you automatically use the five senses you are born with. Then as you get bigger you look to your parents, family and friends for guidance and support, you begin to think, feel, and behave in a way that is acceptable to your upbringing. Just as mine was when I was constantly told I wasn't good enough - I eventually believed that and it showed up in my everyday life.

Your self-image is the way you see yourself in your imagination (sub-conscious) your self-image is so powerful because your behaviour reflects that. I call it your internal guide. This guide is constantly telling you how to behave and act in line with who you think you are. Many people don't even think they have an image of themselves until they look closer. If you continually see yourself as unattractive then you're sending the wrong messages to your unconscious mind and nothing you do will change that - people will see you as unattractive and it becomes a self-fulfilling prophecy.

If you get more than you believe you are worth then the chances are you will lose it because your internal guide is constantly working to instructions about who you think you are.

You will have heard the saying "work hard, play hard" well it's true – some people who earn large amounts of money or inherit it will spend it as quickly as they can or find another way to rid themselves of this money.

Celebrities who rise to stardom quickly can all too often be brought back to earth because of their limiting self-image; there are so many celebrities today with self destructive images and others follow them.

So in a nutshell how you think of yourself will affect how other people feel about you because over 95 per cent of what we communicate is subconscious. People are constantly reacting to one another through the messages transmitted from body language to your tone and emotional signals – they all have an impact in your daily life. You can change your own self-destructive behaviour today by making a few simple changes about your own self image.

Start with a simple evaluation of who you think you are. You may not like what you see but remember you can change it in a heartbeat.

So who are you really?

Underneath is our real self or the authentic self – who we really are. Piled on top of that is all the fear, shame and our negative self image. Then there is another layer that is the person we pretend to be so people will like us.

The final layer of is all people ever get to see of us, we continually strive each day to make certain no one ever sees the other us, the one we are afraid we are underneath it all.

Once you begin to unearth the real you, you can take complete charge of your life and get to have more fun, love, and happiness in your life.

Ask yourself these questions:

Your pretend self: The image you project to the world

A

- How do you like to be seen?
- What part of your personality do you hope people will notice first?
- What is so important that people have to know about you?
- If your life were trying to prove something about you, what would it be?

Your negative self image:

B

- What is the opposite of each of the traits of your pretend self?
- What secrets do you have that no one will ever know?
- Who do you dislike the most and why?

Most perception is projection
OR
We most dislike in others what we fear
can be seen in ourselves!

The real you: your authentic self:

C

- Who you really are always feels natural - a bit like coming home?
- Who are you when no-one is looking?
- If you felt safe in your life what would you do differently?
- Who or what would you be if you could live beyond failure?

By using the above three selves to identify your true authentic self and banish the pretend ones you will begin slowly to live your life more and more from who you really are, the you that is all empowering, wonderful and deserving.

Here is an example of how you can instantly empower yourself. Ask this simple question: Who am I when no one is looking? And try to live your life this way.

It's so simple yet so powerful I guarantee you will begin to see differences in your attitude and behaviour not just towards yourself but towards others as well.

Human behaviour is made up of habit and imagination and is definitely more powerful than logic and willpower.

Your body will respond far more easily to imagination than to simple commands. That's why the way we see ourselves in our imagination is a reflection of how we live our lives.

As Buddha said: "*The Mind is everything that you think you become*".

Simply follow the instructions on the next page to empower yourself and reprogram your mind for success.

Reprogram Your Mind Now

1. Find somewhere comfortable where you can relax
2. Take some really deep breaths until you feel your whole body relaxing.
3. Close your eyes and visualise another you standing in front of you - really get into this scene. This other you has to be the most gorgeous you imaginable.
4. Make the colours big, bright and bold and pull them in really close.
5. Take a few moments to familiarize yourself with that gorgeous other you, noticing what the other you is wearing, how you hold your body and the smile on your face.
6. Notice how that other you handles problems with ease and goes for goals easily.
7. Now I want you to step into that other you and feel the difference. See through the eyes of the other you, hear through the ears of the other you, feel how good it feels to be at one with the real, authentic you.
8. To reinforce this place your index finger and thumb together of your right hand and squeeze them tight. When your feelings are really strong this will reinforce the good feelings and all you have to do is simply squeeze them together whenever you want to get that feeling back again.
9. Keep repeating these reprogramming sessions daily so they sink into your unconscious and become new healthy habits.

Remember as you practice doing these visualization techniques it will become easier and easier as each day goes by.

You will get stronger and stronger in your new found happy, confident self so make that commitment today to align with your authentic self and see as all your hopes and dreams unfold before you.

Some Quotes That I Think You Will Like!
Try to keep at least one of them in mind daily.

- "It is our light, not our darkness that most frightens us."
- "Our deepest fear is that we are powerful beyond belief."
- "You are a child of the universe. Playing small doesn't serve the world."
- "There is nothing enlightening about shrinking so that other people won't feel insecure around you."
- "We ask ourselves; who am I to be brilliant, gorgeous, and talented? Actually who are you not to be?"

"We are born to manifest the glory of the universe that is within us. It's not just in some of us: it is in everyone. And as we let our own light shine, we unconsciously give other people permission to do the same"

MARIANNE WILLIAMSON

Remember: truly brilliant people accept their successes so that they can shine and show others hope.

3

Emotions

We all respond to our emotions differently. In fact we can watch the same programme or see the same event but we will have completely different experiences.

Suppose two different people were going on holiday and were about to board a flight. One of those people was excited and the other not - the difference in both cases is their emotional states.

Emotions such as love, anger, hate, fear, curiosity and hesitancy are just some of the emotional states we are constantly going in and out of every day of our lives and they are all different and unique.

A more simple way to put this would be the mood you're in at any one time is simply your neurology at work. Some of these states don't work in our favour and can become troublesome if we don't recognise when they are happening.

We have all experienced depression, anger and fear – Actually your brain only has two real fears - sound and heights, the rest are all learned experiences from your past. And if they are learned they can be unlearned.

More helpful states would be hope, joy, pleasure, confidence, determination, love, happiness and optimism – these are all quite resourceful states that we should experience more of in our lives.

Think of all human behaviour as a result of the emotional state you're in at any one time.

Internal Representations

**The pictures and sounds we make in our mind
And how we make them**

Anything you have ever done that was magnificent was a result of your emotional state at the time.

Today I want you to experience more of the states you want to be in and more often.

Feelings And Where They Come From

When something happens in our lives we react to it through our emotional state and we can change these emotional states automatically.

Example:

Imagine someone you are attracted to just walked in the room. If you are like most people you will have changed states automatically.

Most of the time we are not aware of the feelings we generate from one moment to the next. Unbeknown to you there is an internal process going on in the gap between the event and your reaction to it.

33

Our Physiology

We constantly affect the states we are in through our body, slight changes in our posture, breathing and facial expressions – they all affect our behaviour. If you make some simple changes to your body language you will have a completely different experience on this planet.

Whatever you're doing I want you to stop for a moment and straighten up your shoulders, hold your head high and put a big smile on your face. Now try to think of that unpleasant situation without changing your posture.

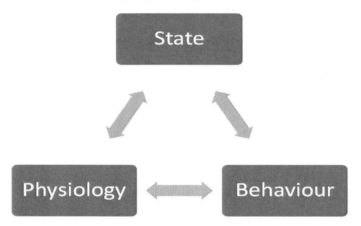

If you've done exactly that; then you will probably notice your feelings have changed, or your feelings about the situation have changed for the better. Remember if you're tense your body is producing different kinds of chemicals to those than when you're relaxed and smiling.

Representational Systems

Also known as sensory modalities or in the NLP world known as the 4-tupe is a neuro-linguistic-programming model that examines how the human mind processes information.

How we feel is determined through the pictures we make in our minds and the way we talk to ourselves in our head. We refer to these images as internal representations and they are just that, representations of our own reality not reality itself.

Your own internal representation is unique to you, think of it as your own way of preserving the world around your personal map of the world. But like any map it will have generalizations, deletions and distortions and so it is incomplete.

This is why, as we mentioned before, two people who can witness the exact same event can experience it completely differently. In NLP there is a saying that "the map is not the territory". Sometimes people will say to me "I can't visualise" but really everyone can visualise. I can prove this answer with the following questions:

- What is the colour of your car?
- What colour hair does your boss have?
- What did you do on your last holiday?

To answer any of these questions you will have had to go inside your imagination and make pictures. We call this visual. Now I know for most people these pictures won't be clear or high quality but that's a good thing because if they were you wouldn't be able to tell the difference from that and the real world.

We also have the ability to talk to ourselves inside our heads and make sounds (Hear). Think of a song that you love, or the sound of the sea. On the other scale can you remember an argument with someone and hours or days later you still play all the nasty things they said to you that make you feel even worse.

Imagine you have been asked to stand in on a meeting with some of your least favourite people, imagine them all talking bullshit and looking at you as if you were a piece of furniture. How much do you want to go to that meeting?

Bad Images

Now imagine your boss, whom you like, asks you to stand in on a meeting with people you like and respect and everyone is excited to see you, everyone is having fun and laughing. These same people are really interested in what you have to say. How much do you want to go now?

If you just experienced any differences at all you will have just recognised how the quality of your internal representations will determine the quality of your life. Yet too many people pay little attention to these interpretations inside their own mind. That is a perfect example of your brain running you, rather than you running it.

Recently I worked with a really gorgeous looking guy who thought he was ugly and didn't have a good physique. I wasn't surprised because of all the pictures he was making inside his head – no wonder he felt so dreadful.

He was a little overweight but had the most gorgeous big blue eyes, chiselled nose, full lips and brilliant white straight teeth – how could he think he was not good enough? Well he did directly through his own thought processes. Once we had worked through some of his issues and I taught him some simple yet powerful techniques to see himself more each day as a powerful creator of his own destiny, he began to see not just himself but the world around him in a different light.

He began to have more and more confidence in everything he did and how he approached life, he was able to lose the unwanted weight he had piled on and look at himself in the mirror each morning with love and gratitude for who he really was rather than who he thought he was.

You see, once he had made the changes on an unconscious level he was able to fix his problems easily after having had years of therapy that only deals with conscious ability. He was in despair of ever getting the help he needed or if he would ever feel right again.

Good Images

If you're experiencing these unhelpful images and sounds in your own mind then do these simple little exercises now to change them forever.

As you learn how to do this more and more you will gain control consciously and subconsciously.

Think now of a bad experience or someone who you don't particularly like and notice every detail as you look at the pictures in your imagination. Maybe the person's face or voice annoys you. Now ask yourself this:

- Is it in colour or black and white?
- Can you see it more to the left or the right of your visual field or right in front of you?
- Is the image big or small?
- Bright or dark?
- Still or moving?

Try out some new ways of changing these images and see

what happens.

1. If your image of the person is moving. Freeze the picture so it is still
2. If the image has any colour, drain out the colour and make it look like a black and white picture.
3. Make the image small like a postage stamp.
4. If it's close up to you, move it out and further away so you can hardly see it.
5. Dress it up and give the person or event a funny hat and a big red nose or paint their face like a clown with no clothes on so they are naked.
6. Now all you have to do is imagine the sound of their voice and change it to something naughty or silly, make it squeaky or funny.

If you have followed all these instructions then you will have collapsed all the old unhelpful representations about that person or event that used to bother you.

You are experiencing powerful changes from 'Unleash The Genius Within' that will help you each day to become more positive in every area of your life. You are becoming the master of your own emotions and reprogramming your mind.

The next time you find yourself in the same situation or see the person you had previously felt badly about, you will feel completely differently, which means they will respond differently to you, changing your future relationships forever.

So remember: Images that are bigger, brighter and bolder have more intensity than those that are dimmer, duller and distant.

Dissociation

Another amazing technique you are about to learn is called Dissociation simply meaning to dissociate from a memory. An–

other way to think of it is to step inside or outside of a memory.

1.   Think of a stressful situation or something that makes you feel uncomfortable.
2.   When you begin - what images come into your mind? Step out of yourself so you can only see the back of yourself. Pull yourself away from the image as far as possible so you are actually pulling yourself out of the picture but you can still see yourself from a distance. This process reduces the intensity of the feeling the image was giving you.

Association

Now we can do the same thing only the other way round; this time you are going to step inside the picture and intensify the good feelings associated in it. This is called Association.

1.   Think of a time when you felt really wonderful and allow an image to come to mind.
2.   Step into the image and fully associate with it so you are seeing with your own eyes, hearing with your own ears and feeling the wonderful sensations in your own body.
3.   Remember to make them bigger, brighter, and bolder and the feelings stronger.

So remember to reduce the intensity you have to step out and move backwards and to intensify step in and make it bigger.

These techniques are so simple but yet so powerful you will master them all quickly and easily.

The power of internal representation can turn you into a highly successful person in a matter of months so don't get left behind; it's your turn to shine.

Now that you know how to influence your own mind you don't have to worry about other people or circumstances to make you feel a certain way. By taking full control of your own mind by the things you say and the way you say them to yourself and the way you use your body, you can begin to feel fully in control of any situation.

4

Your Inner Critic

Nothing makes you feel worse than a well-meaning friend, partner or even a stranger who is willing to criticise you but the worst critic of all is yourself. The way in which you talk to yourself has a lasting effect on your emotional well being.

An example of this would go something like this; when you make a mistake or feel let down for not sticking to a diet what is the tone of your voice and what exactly do you say to yourself? Is it, "oh well I'll try harder tomorrow" or "I'm not going to ever get involved again with that, I can't do it I'm not clever enough"; or is it something like "you stupid idiot, you really are pathetic aren't you? When are you ever going to learn?"

Go on, remember now the last time you did something wrong or made a huge mistake. Remember what you said to yourself. What was your tone of voice? Was it sarcastic, cocky, and angry? So many of us presume that because we have a voice inside our heads that we don't have any choice but to listen to it but I disagree because what is it they say about criticism being constructive? So if your own inner voice is not supporting you fully then try this simple technique to quieten the inner critic.

1. Stop for a moment and talk to yourself the way you normally would with your inner critic saying all those nasty things to yourself in an unpleasant tone of voice.
2. Notice where that voice is coming from.Is it inside your head or outside your head? Is it at the front or the back or the sides?
3. Pull out your arm and stick out your thumb.
4. Where the critical voice is, move it down your arm to the tip of your thumb, so that it can now speak to you from there.
5. Now I want you to slow the voice down and change the tone - make it sound quite sexy or even bewitching or speed it up to sound like a mouse.

This makes it sound much less over-powering or threatening doesn't it?

You must remember though that it's so easy to change your inner critic's voice but the intention of the inner voice is positive – to stop you from making mistakes and help you to do things in a better way.

Imagine if, when you were a child, your parents continually shouted at you and told you how useless you were, you would very quickly lose confidence in your abilities.

However if the same parents continually praised you for everything and told you how good you are with enthusiasm and confidence then you would have a totally different experience.

1. Remember that time you made a big mistake and you criticized yourself badly.
2. Ask yourself - how could I say the same thing in a more helpful way?
3. Go back into yourself at the time you made the mistake and this time

make it different. Give yourself some praise and look for the positives
- cut yourself some slack.

For the next ten days I want you to pay attention and notice
the way you talk to yourself and be fully aware in any moment
what you say and how you say it to yourself.

You have choices. You are in control.

> *"We can't solve problems by using the same kind of*
> *thinking when we created them"*

ALBERT EINSTEIN

Are you a pessimist or an optimist? The difference is crucial.

> *"A pessimist sees difficulty in every opportunity. An optimist*
> *sees the opportunity in every difficulty"*

WINSTON CHURCHILL

5

Super Confidence

Take some deep breaths and hold your head high, pulling your shoulders all the way back so they are nice and straight. Imagine Ki, your life force energy, streaming down from above into the top of your head. This energy is like a laser of white light travelling from the top of your head throughout your whole body and as it enters your body you feel a sense of great pleasure as you become one with the universe.

We all have life force energy. The Chinese call it Chi, the Japanese call it Ki and the Indian yogis call it Paraná. I like to call it Ki for its simplicity. All of these cultures use the life force energy for healing and greater life expectancy; you too will learn about how to use your own life force energy to heal yourself.

Now I want you to remember a time in your life when you felt amazing, totally confident and happy with yourself, if you can't remember such a time then just imagine what it would be like to feel amazing.

Fully return to it now and feel the pleasant sensations

and experience it once more: hear the things you heard and see the things you saw. Now make them bigger, brighter, and bolder. Allow the feelings to intensify and your confidence to sky rocket.

I want you to give your confidence a colour; maybe your favourite colour and keep intensifying the feelings until they are so strong. Then I want you to press your thumb and index finger of your right hand together and squeeze them tight. Wait until the feelings are really strong before pressing the finger and thumb together and hold it for a moment or two before releasing them.

Go ahead and do it now then come back and press your thumb and finger together again to instantly re-experience the same feelings of confidence and pleasure. All you have to do is repeat this simple technique whenever you need a boast of confidence. Repeat the steps as often as possible.

Never underestimate the power of your own mind it works every time.

> *"Continuous effort - not strength or intelligence -*
> *is the key to unlocking our potential"*

WINSTON CHURCHILL

You have all heard of associational links, it is like when you first brought your dog home as a puppy - it needed to be taught many things like going outside to the toilet and when to eat etc... You may even have taught it some other amazing things but for now just imagine you wanted to teach it to eat food at a certain time. You would ring a bell or something similar each time you wanted him to eat his dinner.

After keeping up this association for a few weeks your dog only needs to hear the bell and it will respond to the bell positively by eating his dinner even though there is no logical connection.

Through constant repetition a neurological connection was created in the mind of the dog. Similarly, as humans we can associate things in our own lives so let's create an associational link to instantly having confidence whenever or wherever you need it.

Go back to the time when you felt amazing and confident as above – when you press your thumb and forefinger together to make the experience resurface again. Do it now. Press them together once again and you should easily be able to bring the feelings you had at the time back in full force.

This is your very own associational link to feeling instantly amazing. The more you keep repeating this action the more hardwired it will become in your brain. The mind is very sensitive and will obey your commands at will.

Whenever you find yourself in a stressful or emotional state that you don't like, just follow the same process pressing your thumb and forefinger together of your right hand and you will have a burst of instant confidence and energy.

Turn On Your Charisma

Have you ever met someone who you were instantly drawn to? Could you put your finger on why they had this affect on you? How, when they walked into a room they attracted your attention immediately as if they had a halo shining above their head, or the whole place lit up in their presence.

A lot of high profile people aren't particularly good at their jobs but something about them draws people in – this is what we call charisma.

People who have charisma feel comfortable in their own skin – they are content with whom and what they are, they are not constantly looking for approval from other people.

This is why we like such people in the first place because we feel comfortable around them. Now I'm going to teach you a couple of techniques to make you feel more appreciative of yourself and get that charisma working for you.

The Charisma Switch

Close your eyes and let your breathing slow down taking some deep breaths as you sit or lie in a comfortable position. Drift in the memory of the last time someone paid you a compliment or said something wonderful about you.

Really look at that person and what they said at the time and identify with what it is they love so much about you. Momentarily float out of your body and into the body of the person who paid you the compliment. Now from here you can see yourself standing there looking wonderful and feeling great. When the feelings are as strong as they can be, use the thumb and finger of your right hand technique once again to fully appreciate your wonderful self.

Stay for a few moments and really appreciate what it is about you that they love then fully return to your own self and step out. Sometimes people don't see what it is about them that others love or like, so this is a good way to start seeing your own qualities.

Repeat these exercises as often as possible and you will be surprised at how quickly your confidence and charisma shines through and you will find yourself doing things which previously you could only have dreamed.

6

Emotional Intelligence

By now you will have learned that by modifying your body language you can influence your feelings to act accordingly. The way we talk to ourselves and the pictures we make in our mind.

When you work through your feelings you are learning to use your emotional intelligence. An emotion is a bit like someone knocking at your door. If it is an important message and you don't answer then the knock will get louder and louder until the door breaks down. The message that needs to be delivered will not go away until you respond to it. Then it becomes part of your knowledge and understanding.

Unfortunately western society has ignored or suppressed our emotions and in some cases we never learn to address our emotions properly. Yet understanding our emotions and how to handle them from the moment we are born is a big part of growing up.

You only need to pay attention to the emotions that carry important messages and the easiest way to recognise them is they don't go away, they keep coming back time and time again - just like the knocking on your door.

The ones that are not important tend to vanish and never return, so now you can learn to recognise the difference in your own emotions and start to address them one by one.

So next time your emotions try to deliver a message, pay close attention and answer it, then it will be gone for good so it leaves you free to get on with other more important things in your life.

The Successful Mind

When I decided to change my life the one thing that really stuck me was how little I actually did towards the life I craved. I would rush home from work to do my daily exercise, rush my dinner and fall into bed exhausted each day - that was all I did each and every day.

As a therapist I was helping others with all manner of problems yet I couldn't help myself. I was burnt out, so I decided then and there to change all of that.

If I was going to help people I needed to be able to help myself so everything that I needed to change in my own life I set about doing from that day. I realised I had become trapped in a lifestyle I didn't want and from that realisation everything began to change.

First I lost weight and kept it off by going on a really healthy diet. This was not dieting through starvation but by addressing my own emotional eating that had been present for several years. I found it easy from there as I could recognise when I was emotionally hungry and when I was truly physically hungry. I also began to chew my food slowly - it's a known fact we in the west eat too quickly without allowing our body clock time to send the signals to the brain to tell us when we are full. This in itself had a huge impact on my life.

Each day I found I could focus more on my goals and it felt amazing. I even found time to really enjoy life. I love walking and through the simple meditation techniques that I have shared with you in this book I suddenly found that my life was really going places. I felt fantastic and full of life and energy. I was inspired to move forward in every way.

I want you to be inspired each day of your life so that you get to have more joy, happiness and fun.

Negative Emotions

Everyone gets negative emotions from time to time but some get them more frequently than others. They are simply messages sent from your mind to your body to alert you to something that needs your attention.

An example might be when you are going on a journey. Your mind might play images of what the journey could have in store or things which could happen; it is alerting you for all eventualities so you are well prepared.

Acting On Your Messenger

So in turn I might make a mental list of things I can do to stop those things from happening on my journey, I can prepare for it.

Switch Off the Messenger

It's a bit like switching off the alarm system or hanging up the phone. When I've taken notice of the message from my mind I can drain the colour from it so it becomes less intense, I can also shrink it to the size of a postage stamp and push it away in the distance. If any pictures or images pop back into my mind it simply means I haven't resolved a message and it's trying to tell you to go back and try again. Once you have gone back and resolved any other situations or messages then the images will no longer be there.

Re-Program Your New Future

Now you can really get to grips and imagine the events leading up to your journey or any forthcoming events with enthusiasm, making sure you imagine everything going exactly the way you want. Once again make the pictures bigger, brighter and bolder – full colour and close up so you really feel like it's already done.

Give it a go. Test yourself now... think of something that makes you feel bad and notice what kind of images come into your mind.

As you pay attention to that image, notice:

- Is it a big or small image?
- Is it in colour or black and white?
- Is it a movie or still picture?
- Is there any sound with it?
- Is it in front, of you, or behind you or to the side?

STOP!

This information is what gives the bad feelings their power and you were unconscious of it going on until a few moments ago.

So now you are fully aware of it, we can ask it its intention – what message is it trying to give to you? Take a little time to think through some ways you can solve the problems. Then drain the entire colour from the images and shrink them back to a postage stamp size and move them further away until they are in the far distance.

Then imagine your life. How would you ideally like it to be? What do you most desire? How will you get it? With every new habit it becomes easier to follow these exercises and change your life forever.

Your own thoughts will take on a new meaning as they become richer and have more quality. It's always healthier to think big than too small and to think more often about the kind of things you want to attract into your life.

7

Positivity and Why It's Important

Can you remember a time in your life when you were really confident and happy? It could be from your childhood, the more recent past or even ten years ago? It doesn't matter what the memory was, as long as it was a really happy one.

Now I want you to go back to that time in your mind and fully let go as if it was happening all over again, see what you saw, hear what you heard and feel all the good feelings associated with it. If you don't have any happy memories, then just use your imagination and think about how good it would be to feel totally happy and confident.

- As you go through the images make them bigger, brighter and bolder and the feelings stronger.
- When these feelings are strong, place your thumb and finger of the right hand together and squeeze them tight together.
- Now, release them and open your eyes. Wait a few seconds before going back into the memory one more time.
- Go back to the same memory and squeeze the thumb and finger of your right hand and really get those strong feelings but this time also imagine the rest of the day going just as you want it to with complete

confidence.
- Well done! You have just reset your mind's operating software.

I'm always inspired myself when I meet people who just seem to look at things in a positive light as if they were born with this ability to turn things into a positive. One such person is my best friend Misty, she has always had the most amazing confidence in any human being I've ever witnessed.

No wonder she became famous and an inspiring author of many books. She saw what she wanted and worked each day towards her dream until she looked at her life and had got much more than she originally desired.

You too can have this same ability and make all your dreams become a reality.

Start today learning the art of reframing some of your own situations. Maybe it's something someone at work has said to you or family or friends, it doesn't really matter what or who said it – I just want you to re-frame it to something better.

Example:

If your boss says "why haven't you finished that letter yet?" instead of thinking you're incompetent say "well I just want to make sure we get it right" and make sure you answer all his questions. Of course when you do present the finished letter to your boss he will be blown away with how well you have done it.

Remember there's no such thing as "failure". Failure is an attitude not an outcome.

"If we did all the things we are capable of we would literally astound ourselves"
"Just because something doesn't do what you planned it to do doesn't mean it's useless"

THOMAS EDISON

"Be miserable. Or motivate yourself.
Whatever has to be done, it's always your choice."
"Everything you are against weakens you.
Everything you are for empowers you."
"I cannot always control what goes on outside.
But I can always control what goes on inside."

WAYNE DYER

Start empowering your own life now by asking yourself these questions

- What do I really want?
- Who makes me feel alive?
- What makes me feel good?
- What makes me feel empowered?
- What do I look like when I'm most happy?

As you start to answer all these questions you will build up an image. This is the time to do the finger and thumb exercise as you vividly play each one in your mind until you are happy with it. Press the thumb and finger together of your right hand and stay with the image for a few moments then come out and follow on to the next one.

You will soon build up these positive emotions and keep

repeating them until they become instilled in your mind like second nature (hard wired) then you don't even have to think about them, they will happen automatically for you throughout the rest of your life.

You can even use a positive phrase or quotation that you feel a connection with. Either choose your own or use one from this book and just repeat the phrase as often as you like. It will soon become hard wired into your subconscious mind.

I remember when I first started doing hypnosis and was asked to do a live session. Even though I had never done it before I knew I could do this but I was still nervous and thought "what if people think I'm not good enough". In the end I just thought "well I'm gonna do it" and I used all the techniques I had been taught such as imaging everything going well and seeing myself hypnotising the person easily and with confidence.

Now because I had sent a different message to my subconscious that's exactly what happened – everything went smoothly and I hypnotised them just as I had imagined in my mind plus I was invigorated and on a high from my success.

Next time you find yourself in a situation where you once would have felt uncomfortable or nervous then try this for yourself, it works every time.

- Sit or stand in a comfortable position
- Breathe deeply and relax
- Bring the fear of the event into your mind
- Now make the picture smaller, further away, drain the colour from it.
- Make sure you're outside the picture.
- Now make a big, bright image of the event or situation you were dreading in a different way.

- Make sure you're in the picture now.
- Pull it in close and make it bold and bright.
- See everything going the way you want it to. See your happy smiling face speaking with confidence with your shoulders back.
- Notice how other people react to you differently now you have this amazing confidence.
- Keep playing the image until it's so strong then place your thumb and finger together of the right hand and associate all those good feelings there.
- Now open your eyes and come on out.

Now the next time you place your thumb and finger together you will instantly feel confident and ready to go.

Have you ever failed? If you answered 'no' to that question then you have obviously stopped learning. If you have stopped learning then you have not lived.

People don't fail. Only choices, plans, and strategies fail. The people who make it have made more mistakes than those who don't.

So what do you do if your plan fails? Change your plan or strategy until you find one that works.

Fear of failure is a pointless task, all it can do is hold you back but it can begin to lose its power over you when you change your mindset. I want you all to choose something in your own life that you're having difficulty with and actually allow yourself to fail or to just be wrong about something.

You'll obviously have to decide what failure is for you – remember we all define failure differently, so this week allow yourself to fail at least five times and be proud of it. Once you realise that failure is a stepping-stone to success, the success will be all the sweeter when you've worked hard to get it.

Positivity and why it's important

*"Anyone who has never made a mistake
has never tried anything new"*

ALBERT EINSTEIN

8

Start Creating Your Own Future - NOW

If I am working with private clients or even corporate clients I usually ask this question. If you carry on doing what you're doing now will you succeed?

Shockingly they always seem to know the answer and usually the answer is "no".

One of the biggest differences I've noticed about success and failure is how many people continually look to the past instead of the future. If you look towards the future as your blueprint for success you will eventually get there. After all, the past is the past and it has no significance on your future because you cannot change it but you can change your future.

It's not important how much you have struggled or how many times you've tried to succeed because you are here in the present and you have all the resources inside you that you will need to succeed.

New Beliefs

Let's train your unconscious mind through this simple but powerful exercise to begin operating in a more positive way.

Choose a belief that you think could make a real difference in your life now. Now imagine yourself standing in your own front room having this new belief, make it strong, powerful and real. Step into the picture and feel what you feel and go through what these new beliefs can do for you. When the feeling is at its strongest, press your finger and thumb together on your left hand. This will reinforce the good feelings on an subconscious level.

Remember – fear can make you feel miserable and stop you from what you're trying so hard to do but if you can, learn these simple techniques to collapse the old thought patterns – you will already begin to feel empowered.

"Any intelligent fool can make things bigger, more complex, and more violent. It takes a touch of genius and a lot of courage to move in the opposite direction."

ALBERT EINSTEIN

Future Dreams - Discover Ways to Get What You Want

Who or what makes you feel good about yourself most?

When you begin to answer this question you will automatically start to feel better about yourself on all levels. Now let's make that feeling bigger, bolder and closer.

When you do this, make the feelings associated with it more intense and stronger, notice where the feelings get stronger and give them a colour, this can be your favourite colour or just choose a warm colour appropriate to what you're trying to achieve. Now spin this colour in front of your eyes with both hands all the way down to the soles of your feet, allow the warm feeling to absorb your whole body and now keep spinning for a few moments then stop.

Who or what makes you feel unconditionally loved?

Again let's make the feelings stronger. Make the images bigger, brighter and bolder, the sounds louder and closer. Now again give them a colour, either your favourite colour or a nice warm colour and spin the feelings associated with it from your eyes to the soles of your feet and allow the warm sensation to permeate your body again… again step into what makes you feel unconditionally loved.

Who or what in your life makes you feel richest?

Once again make those feelings stronger, bigger and brighter, the colours bolder and the sounds richer, until you feel it resonate through your whole body again and again. Now give them a colour, once again the colour should be either your favourite colour or a nice warm colour associated with what makes you feel richest. Fill your whole body with the colour and spin it from your head to the soles of your feet and feel what makes you feel richest.

Who or what in your life makes you feel inspired?

You can now use the same format to amplify these feelings of inspiration by making the images bigger, brighter and bolder, the sounds louder and the feelings stronger. Give them a colour and notice where the feeling starts and where it is strongest. Spin the colour from the top of your head to the soles of your feet and step into a feeling of inspiration.

Whilst you're in a state that makes you feel empowered

like this, think about the rest of the day and week ahead and with your imagination visualise everything going smoothly just as you like them to be. See what you'll see, hear what you'll hear, and feel how wonderful it feels to be in control. As you keep building on this super state of awareness day-by-day you will feel more confident in your abilities to take control of your whole life.

Congratulations!

You have just re-programmed yourself to have a great week!

Below the consciousness of your mind is your subconscious mind and that is the part of your personality we want to influence through our new thought patterns. In order that we can make things more concrete, consider this: any idea may be planted in the subconscious by repetition of thought empowered by your total commitment and faith.

You might ask: "Can this be true through demonstration or observation or, is there a method by which the proof can be seen and if there is, is it available to everyone?" The answer is quite simply - yes.

As human beings we tend to not to believe something unless we see it for ourselves. This book is written so you will discover for yourself through reputation of these powerful techniques.

You have all the mental tools necessary to attract abundance into your life, therefore it is absolutely necessary to not only visualise what you want but to believe it with every fibre of your body and soul.

Lack or limitation is but an illusion, prosperity consciousness knows no limitations. It is what you tell yourself: what you believe you are worth and if you are to have all you desire you must know with complete faith you deserve it.

Lift the lid on your beautiful mind now to all the possibilities available to you.

9

Your Personal Genie

"Ask and it is given"

Start using your personal genie today. When you ask the universe for something, it will without question be given.

For centuries there has been a select group of people who are the real thinkers. These people have always known there is a power which penetrates and fills the spaces of the cosmos and that everything you see around you is an expression of that power. The power operates in a very precise manner, which is generally called law. In other words, everything comes from one source and that source power always flows and works to and through the individual – that is you. Stated slightly differently, the image that you have formed can only come to you on the physical plane of life (your results) in one way, and that way is by law and through faith.

"If you can show me a person who achieves great things, I can show you a person who has great faith in his God-given ability to achieve what he his imagination sees." In fact, there is absolutely no question in my mind that faith in one's abilities has always been the miracle worker throughout history. In truth, it is the cornerstone to everything you will ever build or achieve during the course of your entire lifetime.

Comparatively few people today realise just how much faith in oneself (that part of oneself which is spiritual, perfect) has to do with success and achievement, because the great majority of people never seem to

View faith as being a genuine creative force. Yet the truth is that not only is faith a bonafide power but it is the greatest one we will ever experience. In fact, I would go so far as to say that whatever you accomplish in your lifetime, will be in direct proportion to their faith.

Whatever you ask of the universe will be given!

"The most beautiful thing we can experience is the mysterious.
It is the source of all true art and science. He to whom this
emotion is a stranger, who can no longer pause to wonder and
stand rapt in awe, is as good as dead: his eyes are closed"

ALBERT EINSTEIN

Attitude for Success

When you change, the world around you changes too. You will notice that you begin to attract positive people into your life. Once you become more confident other people will notice these changes. The change in your thinking will also change your behaviour towards yourself and others causing a ripple effect throughout your whole life.

As your attitude has changed this also causes things in your everyday life to change. Now for some this causes a sense of panic and fear. If you are insecure, then the familiar is a far safer bet, no matter how bad things may be.

This is when you have to own your change and give yourself permission to be slightly apprehensive and embrace change. Go for it knowing the outcome will be for the best, if you don't, chances are you'll go back to your old ways not because they are better but because they are safe and familiar.

Example

Nicole was half way through the linguistic code programme when she noticed her partner Phil was not supportive of her and continually called her names making fun of the new pro-gramme she had embraced. Nicole realised that he was not changing with her and that her own development would be stopped if she stayed. Even though Nicole loved him it was not enough to keep the relationship going as the person she loved no longer existed.

The changes you make will amaze you as your new life enfolds before you, allow yourself the freedom to drift and let the images in your mind just flow in and out and really trust your own instincts. There are only three things you need for a super new life:

1. A Dream (A clear direction)
2. A Goal (Your destination)
3. Persistence (Never Give In)

To put it another way:

When you pursue your dreams guided by your goals with clarity and persistence miracles happen!

Fantasy & Dreams

Our dreams are what we live for and we all have them, so why not start to focus more on your dreams daily? Think of what it is you truly want and desire, take your time to really get into the dream and let your mind just wander around for a while.

Whilst you're doing that answer a few questions and see what you come up with; what would you do if you knew you couldn't fail? What would you do if no one was looking? And try to live your life by these questions.

When you do a whole new way of life can open up for you.

> *"Do not let what you cannot do*
> *interfere with what you can do."*
> JOHN WOODEN

> *"In the sky, there is no distinction of east and west;*
> *people create distinctions out of their own minds*
> *and then believe them to be true."*
> BUDDHA

When you have followed the above method you will have done what all truly successful people have done for centuries – used your positive state to access all the creative part of your mind. All the truly great thinkers of our time have used these methods on a daily basis to get what they want purposefully.

People like Albert Einstein saw their vision in the depths of their unconscious long before it became a reality.

For anything to happen in the real world
It first has to happen in the imaginary world.

Please stop for one moment and take a look around you at your surroundings – almost everything you see has started from the seed of thought inside someone's head. In order for you to make improvements in your life, you need to allow yourself to dream.

Some studies show that less than 4% of us write down our goals. We tend to think of it as tedious or time-wasting, instead of just scrambling though life at a fast speed without thought and then wondering why we feel so bad, most people will in fact spend more time making a list of clothes to take on holiday than on the really important things in life. This has to change if you want to succeed.

You wouldn't set off to another part of the country without a road map or a sat nav would you? Simply because you need to know your destination and all the routes you can take to get there safely. If you didn't take a map, you would most probably get lost, so you see that is exactly what's happening now in your life. If you're lost it's because you haven't got a plan and a map to go with it.

Test

Think about what it is you want. Imagine what it would be like to have it. Make sure it's ok to have it without hurting or harming anyone else. Now think about how you can make it happen, focus on all the ways in which you can make it happen. Write down your plans for the future and all the necessary steps you need to take to get there by the quickest and easiest route. Then take steps each day towards that ultimate goal. As time passes you will eventually look back and see just how far you have come.

10

Make It Happen

When I sat down years ago, I asked myself, "If I continue on the present course I'm on, where will I be five years from now?" I was very shocked at what stared back at me, that if I carried on thinking and acting in the way I did, that five years into the future I wouldn't be any more fulfilled or happy.

I took myself through all the techniques I'm sharing with you here in 'Unleash The Genius Within' to change my own life. I went through the visualizations, and tapping techniques that you will learn in this book.

The results were worth the effort because that's one of the reasons I was able to write this book. I immediately began to feel better. I had more energy and suddenly life presented to me endless opportunities in a way I could never previously have imagined.

I attracted the kind of positive people I had dreamed of and was doing the things I had always wanted to, it wasn't just my dreams that were coming true, I was finally living the dream.

Through my own experiences I have taught thousands of

people on my workshops and seminars the following techniques.

The Hidden Dream System

This hidden dream system is different from conventional goal setting because it has a beginning, middle and end. An end result that you get to live your life exactly how you want. In order for you to start doing this it will be absolutely necessary to know or identify your values - those very things that make your life worth living. These will act a bit like a road map and give you a sense of direction for your journey.

Finally when your road map is set for the journey ahead in a clear route, we can focus on other small goals, the little roads on the road to your new brilliant life. This is one of the most important parts of this whole book and you should now grab pen and paper and answer all the questions in full detail. Don't worry too much if you don't get it all right, the universe will still know your sincere efforts and reward you for it.

Stage One

The most important things in your world

What would you do if there was a disaster and the world was about to explode in front of your eyes?

Your answer is an indication to your deep set values, what matters most to you. When I worked with a 45 year old man who had had a stroke and didn't expect to survive, I asked him what he thought about when he was told he had survived. He said he had wished that his life had ended because he didn't want to be a burden on his wife and be a vegetable.

This story is not unlike a lot of other stories I've heard

from people in similar circumstances, can you imagine what you would regret in your own life if you were at the end of it now? I've never heard anyone say I wish I had another big house, shockingly they say things that would have made them laugh more, love more and connect with people on a deeper level, yet we go through life doing the opposite.

Opportunities for an abundant life are all around us on every level, we just need to pay more attention and become more conscious of our lives as we travel through it. When you learn to focus on your life and pursue values instead of just goals, you will automatically begin to feel better, it's a bit like coming home.

Question Time

1. Imagine being at the end of your life. What are the three most important things you've learned and why?
2. Who has had the most impact on your life and why?
3. Who are you when you're at your very best?
4. Who are you when no one is looking?

Now answer the above questions and write down your answers. When you're happy with your answers, ask yourself what was the most important thing you learned about yourself. But make sure you leave out the material things like money etc.

Example

I asked a lady on my training seminar to do the above exercise and she had discovered money to be her most important thing in life, so she imagined what it was like to have loads of it and how her life would be with all this money. When she opened her eyes she said having this money would empower her and earn her respect, people would listen to her. I then asked her "what would having more respect do for you?" and "what would having a feeling of empowerment do for you?" She said I will feel loved and respected, so really the money wasn't the real answer, in fact she discovered what was most important to her was love and respect, and money was just her way of getting it.

Deep down, whether we own up to it or not, we all want to be loved and respected, it is part of our natural emotions as human beings because without it life wouldn't be worth living.

Live your life everyday as if no one was looking

Stage Two

When you think of your success, you need to think bigger, you need to go beyond what's possible, you have to dream the impossible because only then can you make it possible. As George Bernard Shaw said "some men see things as they are and ask why. Others dream things that never were and ask why not?" All true progress depends on the unreasonable man. With your values firmly in mind, now make a list of absolutely everything you want now and in the future. Just sit with pen and paper and get it out. Allow your mind to open up to the possibilities you once never thought possible for you.

It is not necessary to believe in the things you write down just now or even believe you'll achieve them all, so no matter how strange or weird, all I want is for you to write it down! Take at least 10 minutes to do it, go away and come back before moving on to stage three...

Stage Three

Only you know what makes your heart skip a beat and only you know what makes you have a spring in your step. When you start to answer the questions below it's very important to be consciously aware and not consider whether some of it is possible or not, just let your answers flow out...

1. What do you love so much that you'd pay to do it?
2. What are you really passionate about?
3. What would you choose to do if you had unlimited power?
4. Who do you most admire from past or present history and why?

Answering these questions will help you have a view of what you live for and takes limiting beliefs away from your current mindset and lets you be ridiculously creative. If you want more clarity ask yourself these two questions:

1. What was it you wanted to do when you grew up as a child?
2. What interested you most as a child?

Write down whatever comes into your mind, allow thoughts to just come like clouds drifting in and out. You don't even need to be precise or even know how it's going to happen – just let your creative juices flow.

Now think about all the really major areas of your life such as family, friends, career, health, money, relationships.

Again write down whatever comes to mind. You don't have to be specific on anything here just write.

1. If you could have something you thought impossible what would it be?
2. If you thought something was impossible to learn for you what would

it be?
3.   What skills would you like to have?
4.   How much money would you like to have?
5.   What character traits would you like to own?
6.   What would you give back to the world when you get it?

Now I want to get you to start forming your big dream; make sure your dream is exactly what you want and not what you don't want. You would be surprised how many people do this! Now focus on it to the point of being obsessed. You will come to realise that what you focus more on, you get more of – it's that simple.

Your vision of who you want to be is the greatest asset you have. Without having a goal it's difficult to score.

So how good do you want to be ?

Good/Very Good/The Best In Your Field/The Best In The World?

11

You Don't Have To Be Clever Academically

Have you ever noticed how the cleverest people at school are not those who make it? What you learn from school are facts about things and places and people. As you go along, you accumulate these facts and store them in your massive store house (the subconscious mind) the more facts you can remember, the cleverer you become.

Interestingly, those who fail at school are usually not interested in facts or, to put it another way, the facts are not put to them in a way they find interesting. Some people learn differently and as schools go they teach pupils all the same way in the same method and if a child doesn't show signs of improvement they get labelled as having learning difficulties. How bizarre is that? I should know as it happened to me. I simply wasn't taught anything at school simply because my brain understood things in a different way to how they taught you.

When I left school at sixteen I felt insecure and didn't think I was clever enough to do anything much apart from working in a shop and that was probably too good for me. It wasn't until years later that I began to question the silent voice within who I knew would never let me down – my inner voice, my subconscious was actually looking out for me even then and I didn't know it.

My inner voice kept telling me that I could do it, that I was clever and I should do something and show them all that I was right one day.

After all people who are academically clever get jobs on their qualifications (the past), not on their desire to succeed (the future). As long as the goal is there, there are no limits to your achievements.

Example:

From today for the next two weeks try to do things you think you are incapable of.

If you think you're unable to work for one of the best companies in the world, make that your aim.

If you think you're incapable of being the next top model, make that your aim. Simply make your vision of where you want to be a reality.

> *"The way to be nothing is to do nothing.*
> *Most of the important things in the world have been*
> *accomplished by people who have kept on trying*
> *when there seemed little hope"*

DALE CARNEGIE

Whose Fault Is It Anyway?

When you're involved with something that goes wrong, never blame other people for your mistakes. Blame no one but yourself.

If you accept total responsibility, you are in a position to do something about it.

Here are some common excuses for failing:

- I needed a better job anyway.
- I need a new partner anyway.
- There wasn't enough time.
- There wasn't enough money to do it.
- I was too busy with other things.
- I wasn't given enough time

You get my drift. These are very common language patterns we use daily to give ourselves permission to fail. The point is that, whatever other people's failings might be, you are the one to shoulder the responsibility.

There are no excuses

Great Ideas Should be Shared

When I was in China studying Zen and Macrobiotics a great teacher told me something I'll never forget. He said "if you give away everything you know, more will come back to you". I believed him totally. This information led me to a day dream state where I remembered being at school and a young girl I used to sit next to would hoard her work and not want to share it, not because she was cleverer than anyone else but because she thought she was.

You can even find this type of behaviour in the workplace where people won't share their knowledge or information; those people stand out like a sore thumb because usually they want to take all the credit for things well done and not share it with their colleagues.

This becomes a problem because if you hoard, you end up living off your reserves and eventually become stale. If on the other hand you give away everything you have, you are left with nothing. This forces you to look and be aware and replenish. When you continually learn, you continually have more and more. Somehow the more you give away, the more you get back, remember ideas are for everyone they are open knowledge so don't go claiming ownership.

Timeline for Success

Something spectacular always happens when you're on a timeline to success; you will know when you're on track. Just how long do you think it will take to be living the big dream? Six months? One year? Two years? Three years? Now working backwards from when your dream is accomplished, focus on the things you need to do to get there, these are the major things you need to do for your guaranteed success.

Write them all down so you don't get lost en route to your dream life, and remember these are the little steps along your route or roadmap to success. Think now of at least five goals and your timeline to carry them through, try to visualise your goals one by one on a separate timeline, this timeline will let you know you're en route to achieving your dream.

Remember when you're visualising the goal, always make

it bigger, brighter, closer and in full colour. Hearing what you heard at the time, you reach success relishing your new found freedom. Allow yourself to float inside the new successful you each time you do this exercise.

You will need to follow this process on a regular basis – every day if you can is best.

Old Habits Die Hard

What exactly will it take for you to be living your dream? I have lost count how many times I've seen people complain that the only resources they have are either their friends or being a good talker, seemingly forgetting that they have so much more available to them. When they do get stuck it's not because they've run out of options, it's more because they have their habitual blinkers on. Stepping outside your comfort zone is never easy and guess what, it's not meant to be easy, that's the whole point. If you want to be great you have to first think great.

Here are a few pointers in the right direction:
1. Rehearse your achievements in your imagination each day.
2. Visualise from the time you become who you want to be and work backwards to the present time.
3. Become more aware of yourself and your daily surroundings.
4. Examine your beliefs and change them to suit.
5. Motivate yourself each day by using the power of your mind.

"Nothing can stop the man with the right mental attitude from achieving his goal; nothing on earth can help the man with the wrong mental attitude"

THOMAS JEFFERSON

1.   Your Talents, Skills

Example: Honest, Loving, Generous, Funny, Loyal.

2.   Where You Live

- People you work for
- People who work for you
- Neighbours
- Friends
- Customers

3.   Finances

Examples: bank accounts, business, home owner, salary etc.

4.   Things you own

Examples: house, laptop, car, business, etc.

It's always a good idea to list the resources we have because it forces us to see things in a new light and expand our thinking to what more we can do or be! Here is an example of when you will recognise Unleash The Genius Within working for you.

The Dream Machine

"Unless you try to do something beyond what you have already mastered, you will never grow."

Ronald E.Osborn

When we learn or do something new we create a neural link in the brain to make it easy to strengthen the experiences we have created. This is one of the reasons it is of paramount importance to mentally rehearse your success. Some of the most famous actors and actresses I have met have rehearsed and already won their part long before they did it for real.

As you begin to visualise your own dreams every day, you will build a strong neural link of your own and watch as your own success unfolds before you.

Visualise Your Future

Whatever you're doing now just stop and sit comfortably while you begin to visualise what life will look like in the future. What will you see? What will you hear? What will you feel? When you get the picture of this wonderful new future in full colour, you are creating a rich experience as if it were already happening. Make sure you associate fully into the picture and not as an onlooker.

Continue this process mentally for a few moments, you can spend ten minutes or an hour each day doing this or even just do it every other day, it's all up to you but in my own experience it's best to do this every day to really reinforce the link in your mind.

The more you do it, the easier it will become as the images will get clearer and more vivid, just like learning to drive a car when you first start, it seems really hard when you have to remember which foot goes on which pedal and which gear is for what but after you've been doing it for a while everything gets easier and your brain learns to automatically know when to change gear. Then one day you pass your test and the rest is history.

This is exactly what you're doing every time you learn

something new, after much practice it becomes unconscious, meaning you do it without thinking consciously anymore, it's hardwired inside you.

Actions Speak Louder Than Words

Of course, if all you ever needed to do was just start thinking about what you wanted and it magically appeared out of thin air then everyone would be driving around in a Rolls Royce, living in a big house and have the most stunning partners in the world. It would actually be chaos on planet earth, that's why the wonderful universe plays its most clever trick in letting you think what you want and actually getting it - this is what I call the action call. You will probably know someone or have heard of people who sit around all day-dreaming and actually never do anything. However by sending a clear representation of how you want to live your life and focusing on it every day, you will become motivated to take action and you will know where you are going.

Each journey begins with a single step, think of at least two things you can do today on your journey to success and stay focused then just do it!

Remember when each day you take small steps forward you will also begin to notice little incidents as your signals are attracting the things you want into your life. It's a bit like a magnet picking up the signals, the more you focus on them the stronger the signals will get.

"All that we are is a direct result of what we have thought"

BUDDHA

I have found in my own life that luck is more predictable than I once thought, if you want more luck take more chances. Be more active. Show up more often.

> *"Twenty years from now you will be more disappointed by the things you did not do than by the ones you did. So throw off the bowlines. Sail away from the safe harbour. Catch the trade winds in your sail. Explore. Dream. Discover".*

Mark Twain

Keep a track on your personal success each and every day so you know where you're going, just like a map and keep on track.

In the next chapter prepare yourself for the most advanced secret teachings from eastern medicine.

12

Power to Heal

**These secret methods date back over five thousand years –
Harness the most advanced life force skills known to man.**

When I was studying ancient Chinese traditions, I accidentally came across one of the most important secret healing techniques I have ever seen. Why am I sharing it with you? Because it belongs to all of us and I've always believed that if people are armed with the right information and facts then they will make the right decisions in their lives.

Of course, I don't profess to be a conventional medical woman but I don't have to be to understand how my own body works and how I can help it to heal itself naturally. I believe conventional medicine and drugs take away our choices, we can only understand through learning more and more about ourselves and the world around us that there are other more natural ways to help illness and disease.

- Imagine being able to treat and prevent colds, viruses, ulcers, heart disease, arthritis, menopause, impotence - simply by breathing and changing a few simple eating patterns.

- Imagine banishing headaches, fatigue, nervousness, stiffness and pain.
- Imagine harnessing the most powerful force in your body and channelling it.

This is a most amazing discovery because I've been researching natural cures from around the world for over five years. We live in a mad high speed, high tech world and eventually as human beings we will suffer from the effects of that.

I've never seen a treatment or system quite like this one, so please read carefully and help yourself to some of the most amazing healing techniques. It's very rare that westerners will have ever seen or heard of these techniques. It's a secret system used by Chinese/Japanese doctors for everything from colds and flu to heart disease and cancer and I use them in my therapy sessions and the healing code.

The techniques I'm about to share with you are based on a force called" Chi" or "Ki "in China or "prana" in India. Shiatsu and acupuncturists all work on the same life-force principles. In fact, anyone familiar with Eastern forms of exercise and meditation has probably heard of "chi". "Tai ch"i, "yoga", "qi gong", "karate", and "Zen" meditation. All teach correct breathing as the basic necessity for practice. That's because correct breathing focuses the power of chi and radiates it through the body.

I'll tell you more in a moment about this great system but first let's cover why you so desperately need these secret techniques.

Your Breathing Is Probably All Wrong

In the western world we have been taught simple breathing exercises but we haven't been taught that proper breathing is actually a force to be reckoned with. We learn to breath by puffing out our chest, this causes us to take only very shallow breaths by using only the upper part of our lungs and forgetting to use the lower part of ours lungs.

This poor breathing has lead to a condition called "hyperventilation syndrome" a recognised condition in the west that can cause anything from tiredness to chest pain and sexual problems. People who only take rapid upper short breaths are not getting enough oxygen in their body.

Doctors Recognise the Need for Proper Breathing

Any doctor can tell you that exhaling carbon dioxide too quickly will disturb the acidity and alkalinity levels also known as the PH-levels in your blood. When the acid levels drop, it can cause a complicated reaction to occur that stops the blood cells from delivering oxygen to the muscles and organs including the brain.

This can lead to a whole manner of problems from high blood pressure to racing heart rate that can be at the root of many problems including heart disease.

Doctors have begun to recognise the importance of proper breathing. Breathing techniques are used regularly for a whole variety of treatments from sports practice to high blood pressure etc. This is obviously a good start, but western doctors are still only using very simple and outdated techniques to get more oxygen into the lower lungs.

Western medicine completely ignores the most powerful secret of healing...

Western medicine has refused to recognise the power and existence of the energy field, yet we are all made up of energy in every cell of our bodies. If western scientists can't see it or put it under a microscope it simply doesn't exist. Why? Because they need to keep the gravy train of western medicine going, after all if we all suddenly started to understand and use the power within us, then we wouldn't need drugs or the medical profession to help us get better.

Ancient healing systems believe that when "Chi" is installed in your body you become sick. Therefore when you practise these secret techniques your energy can travel freely through-out the body, healing, and preventing disease. That's why "Chi" is used in so many eastern healing arts. They believe that healing and wellness come from the care of central life force, this energy system is within every living thing. The belief is when "Chi" flows freely your body is in a state of harmony and wellness, when "Chi" is blocked illness and disease occur.

In all eastern healing systems they have been using these techniques for thousands and thousands of years and are not bound by western limitations and thousands of years of success is proof enough for them. Probably one of the most well known healing arts known to western man is acupuncture. Acupuncture charts show 12 meridians in the body that "Chi" flows through, as well as other minor meridians across the body. The acupuncturist uses very fine thin flexible needles placed on the points to stimulate Chi (Energy). Accu-pressure and Reiki all work with the body's energy field.

The fact is that all people feel the life force energy every day of their lives. They are just not aware of it. For most of us, the sensations of life force energy cannot be distinguished from the background street noise we hear each day. We have grown accustomed to it and do not notice it anymore. We only notice it when we stop and pay attention. Sometimes, the last things to be noticed are those which are most precious to us. Life force is such a thing. Yet there is a lack of awareness to this wonderful force, however it is easily felt by most without effort.

MBS treatment simply uses simple body postures, simple movements and very precise breathing methods to change the flow of this wonderful powerful Chi inside and outside of the body. One of the benefits of using my system is that you don't need to see an Acupuncturist or Reiki Healer or any other therapist at all. You can practise MBS at home whenever you want - it's that simple.

Simple Techniques to Balance the Mind and Body

Later, one of the first techniques in the MBS system you will learn is how to prepare for MBS by relaxing the body. You will be shown the exact posture for each exercise. These are extremely relaxing and comfortable positions. When you're in the proper position it's called "conditioning your body".

Next you're taught how to relax your mind and body completely, relaxing you in a state of light hypnosis.

The Speed of Breathing

Slower Breathing Techniques (Giving More Yin Energy)

1. **Physically** - Your metabolism slows down; including the heartbeat,

blood circulation and other body fluid circulation. Body temperature is usually affected becoming fractionally lower.

2. **Mentally** - producing a much more tranquil state, and clear thinking and objective understanding, as well as much more sensitivity to the environment.

3. **Spiritually** - developing your perceptions, deeper insight which leads to more universal consciousness.

Faster Breathing Techniques(Giving More Yang Energy)

1. **Physically** - resulting in faster metabolism of different body functions. The heartbeat as well as other bodily functions is accelerated and body temperature is increased.

2. **Emotionally** - Producing a more unstable environment where excitement and emotion is increased.

3. **Spiritually** - developing more subjective and egocentric observations with more attachment to material and learned behaviours.

Depth of Breathing

Shallow Breathing (Giving More Yin Energy)

1. **Physically** - resulting in a less active metabolism and disharmony with various other physical functions including body temperature that can become irregular.

2. **Mentally** - becoming more anxious and unstable which can sometimes lead to fear in people?

3. **Spiritually** - developing shallow perceptions about life, lack of confidence and courage, as well as loss of memory and your vision for the future.

Deeper Breathing (Giving More Yang Energy)

1. **Physically** - giving you more profound energy levels and active metabolism and harmony within the bodily functions. Body

temperature becomes more stable.

2. **Mentally** - giving you deeper satisfaction, emotional stability, much stronger confidence levels.
3. **Spiritually** - developing more caring, thoughtfulness, and embracing more positive thoughts and perceptions about the future.

Length of Breathing

Longer Breathing - Gives More Yin Energy

1. **Physically** - resulting in better co-ordination among the metabolism of various functions. Body temperature is more stable and general health is much better.
2. **Mentally** - producing much more peace and harmony and feelings of satisfaction, with less emotional excitement.
3. **Spiritually** - developing much more thoughtfulness, and a wider understanding of past and present memories.

Shorter Breathing - Giving More Yang Energy

1. **Physically** - having a tendency to create faster and irregular metabolism in various body functions. Body temperature tends to increase slightly.
2. **Mentally** - giving more frequent changes of images and thought processes of the mind. Tendency to become impatient with others and have a much shorter temper.
3. **Spiritually** - causing more disharmony and more conflict with short-sightedness.

According to the above it is therefore recommended that we should maintain a breathing pattern that is ultimately slower, deeper and longer, rather than one that is shorter, faster and shallower.

Breathing is natural to us and there should be no real effort needed to maintain this constant state of wellness.

Therefore when you start to learn these techniques they will quickly become second nature. You can enhance this system even more by adopting a healthier eating plan that consists of more fruits and vegetables that are in accordance with your country.

Secret Breathing Techniques

The Five Star Breathing Technique for complete physical, mental and spiritual development.

1. The Breathing of Health

This very long, quiet and slow breathing technique should be used daily to enhance your natural powers of healing.

Breathe through the nose for both inhaling and exhaling, very quietly so that if you had a feather in front of your nose it would not move. The duration of the out breath should be two to three times longer than the in breath. The effect of this breathing is to calm all the senses including the physical, mental and spiritual activities, so we can enter a deep relaxation and develop inner sight. This breathing also produces the effect of minimizing egocentric delusion. Do this at least three times daily.

2. The Breathing Of Harmony

Normal quiet breathing: this breathing is done through the nose but it is slightly stronger than that above, it is a breathing of stillness and quiet. Again the duration of the out-breath should be two to three times longer than the in-breath. The effect of this type of breathing is to allow peaceful, harmonious relations, keeping the self in a central position, which increases awareness of our surroundings.

3. The Breathing Of Confidence

This breathing is inhaled through the nose and exhaled through a slightly opened mouth. The exhalation is three to five times longer than the inhalation. This type of breathing is stronger than the two mentioned above. It is to activate harmony and confidence through the spiritual and mental functions to prepare you for active movement which can happen at any time. You can then adapt to a rapidly changing environment.

4. Action Breathing

Long, deep, and very strong breathing. This breathing is done through a slightly opened mouth for inhaling and exhaling. This breathing will activate spiritual, mental and physical powers. This type of breathing can also help to release mental stagnation and bring clarity back into your life.

5. 'Hi-Fu' Wind Breathing

This long, deep and powerful spiritual breathing technique is done through an open mouth for both inhaling and exhaling. The exhalation once again should be three to five times longer than the inhalation breath. When you breathe in, the very sharp sound of 'Hi' occurs naturally because of the sharp inhalation between the teeth and relaxed tongue. During exhalation the natural sound of 'Fu' is made continually. The effect of this type of breathing is to activate energy and the physical and mental metabolism and spiritualize your whole being. The sound 'Hi' meaning spirit, fire and sun in a pre-historic pronunciation. Also at that time HI and Fu also had the meanings of one and two.

Remember to practice these special breathing techniques between three to five times daily and you will be amazed at your own transformation.

1. Rise early every day at dawn.
2. Close your eyes and reflect on the day ahead.
3. Stay calm and go through the breathing exercises in this chapter.
4. Eat only natural home grown foods and less fat.
5. Chew your food at least 50 times on each mouthful.

6. Take a walk in the park everyday or if you don't live near a park, a walk around the shops should do.
7. Do exercise each day that will make your heart race. I'll leave that to your own imagination.
8. Be nice to people. If they don't smile give them one of yours.
9. Do something every day towards your goals and stay focused.
10. Have gratitude for your life.

Never underestimate the power of these simple exercises.
They are powerful beyond belief.

13

The Power of Napping

There's no rush to reach the end of your life is there? Well you would think so the way we rush through it at full speed. I'm always amazed at how some of us never let go of the childhood rush of wishing we were older. I remember as a child thinking "I wish I was older then I could do this or that". Well it's all well and good as a child but when I did eventually get older I remember wanting to slow the ageing process down.

The fact is people are always rushing here and rushing there, rushing to get dressed and rushing to get home at the end of the day, some people then sit down and rush to finish their dinner before rushing to get some sleep and never finding time for sexual relations with their partner or when they do, they rush that too. Wow! I feel exhausted after just writing it.

Research has shown however that power naps are good for you, that's why people from Mediterranean countries have a relaxed attitude to life because they have these power naps daily without even thinking about it, they know the innate wisdom that lies within our own bodies to rest and rejuvenate. Our bodies have a cycle of rest and alertness every ninety minutes. This is when the body stops external behaviour and takes fifteen minutes or so to replenish its energy reserves.

We all know this gentle, soft feeling of daydreaming that allows us to momentarily escape before returning to the present, usually refreshed and invigorated with an inner wisdom of knowing what to do. It is quite simply your body's natural stress control mechanism.

It is unfortunate that most people ignore their own body's natural signal to relax and replenish, usually trying even harder by drinking more coffee to stay awake or try to concentrate even harder. Learn to listen to what your own body is telling you and allow this daydream state each day, twice a day, for up to twenty minutes and you will experience the most profound difference in your life.

I often use a deeper state of this relaxation called self-hypnosis by imaging myself walking in the woods surrounded by nature and just listening to what mother nature has to say to me. I usually imagine what it is that I want to have in my life. Given that the imagination does not differentiate between what is real and what is imagined then it's easy to tell your nervous system you already have it. When you do this every day it will soon become a habit and will be hard wired into your subconscious leaving you feeling refreshed knowing your unconscious mind has begun to make the imagined changes become a reality and you feeling ready for anything life has to throw at you.

The good thing is you can practice this relaxation or power nap anywhere anytime without anyone noticing what you're doing. You can do this exact technique through taking some deep breaths and letting your mind just wander away. Drifting, floating and feeling your whole body relax before imagining yourself in your favourite place.

Some of the greatest minds on earth used these power naps to recharge their batteries including Thomas Edison and Albert Einstein.

"There is more refreshment and stimulation from a nap, even the briefest, than in all the alcohol ever distilled."

HK KELLY

As you have already discovered in this chapter, the body doesn't distinguish between an emotional threat and a physical one. So whatever happens, it prepares to protect you by fighting or running away. But very often there is nowhere to run or no one to fight so the body gets all worked up but, as the tension builds, there is no release.

Amazingly though, just as the mind can influence the body, so the body can influence the mind. Once we learn to let go of the tension through physical exercise and meditation it begins to feel calmer, safer and in control. The easiest way to rid the body of this excess tension is through exercise. I know some of you will be thinking 'Oh God no not the dreaded exercises' but it doesn't have to be anything too elaborate. If you're not an exercise person a walk in the park, round the block or anything which makes your heart speed up is enough. Enough said.

If you follow these simple exercises on a daily basis you will enjoy a better life, feel more energized and have more control over everything you do. Are you ready for it?

14

The Little Genie Diet
Power Eating

Power represents our life force energy. When we learn to use this power with consciousness and love, it creates a life of health, happiness and peace. The way you eat affects you mentally, physically and emotionally. This power eating technique will teach you how to experience a greater power than you ever thought possible.

The key to health and happiness is right under your nose, when you stop for a moment each day and consider what it is you want out of life and the changes you would like to make. The power eating technique will help you eat less and improve your digestion. It will also help boost your immune system and increase your life force energy and vitality.

How you eat is just as important as what you eat. This programme is a bit like going back in time, to an era when people only ate to survive but I promise you, if you give it a chance you will be surprised at how much you don't miss the processed stuff that was never meant to be part of our diet. I just think when you know the facts you will make the right choices in your life, so let me help you do just that.

For the past ten years I have helped many people who have tried many different health programmes and diets with poor results. Yet, after learning The Diet Genie and how to eat properly, they begin to improve and rid themselves of the poisons inside their bodies, this included people with illnesses that had plagued them for years.

Health and transformation need a complete discipline and food awareness; I hope you find the inspiration to transform your life because eating well is the greatest gift we can give ourselves.

During my studies into macrobiotics and eastern disciplines, I learned that to chew liquid is possible and that this simple act became my discipline to learn to eat more slowly. Most people believe that twenty to thirty times is enough chewing but I always tell people chew more. Yes, it does feel strange when you first start to do this but it will soon become unconscious if you keep it up and don't give in.

In many countries and traditions around the world eating is considered a very important part of their daily life. Yet all we do now is interrupt our meal time by the telephone ringing or looking at the computer whilst we eat. I've seen mums jumping up and down grabbing food when they can and then reaching for a digestive tablet to ease the pain of eating.

According to consumer spending data, we spend £575 million a year on digestion remedies in the UK. Some people are suffering – are you one of them? If so it's time to take a look at you're eating and your lifestyle habits.

There are obviously several reasons why some people eat an unhealthy diet, most of that is due to lack of awareness and planning. But you don't have to be a victim of unhealthy eating habits. Below you will find a few unhealthy habits that people struggle with.

Too Few Meals in the Daytime

When most people go on diets they tend to skip the meals at one of the most important times of day. Mostly breakfast and even lunch only to fight the overpowering urge to eat late at night which is of course the opposite to what you should be doing. So how do you break this unhealthy cycle?

Include three low calorie meal plans each day in your meals. Total calories for each meal should range between 300 and 400 calories for women and 400 to 600 calories for men. A couple of low calorie snacks between meals such as a fruit, or sugar free low fat yogurt will help fight the temptation to eat unhealthy.

Unawareness of Fat and Sugar Content

Most people eat foods with no idea of their calorie or fat value. This leads to weight gain and unhealthy eating habits because you can consume twice as many calories as you should. If you don't know how many calories you are eating buy a calorie counter. But, I always advise after the first few weeks of getting to know your foods and what portions you should eat, you won't need one. You will be able to tell how much food is on your plate and the fat and sugar content quite easily. Just like everything new you learn, it will become second nature.

Eating Junk Foods.

The problem with eating junk food is it leads to craving more of it. A handful of crisps or chips usually lead to you wanting more. Once you break the cycle of eating junk and unhealthy foods you will find it easier to maintain your weight.

All processed foods contain additives and toxins that are more harmful to your health than you can ever imagine. Stop the chain now and open your eyes to the big food chains who are making millions of pounds from you on a daily basis. Your health is the pay off for this mistake.

There is nothing more annoying for me than to listen to other weight loss programmes and so called experts claiming you can eat whatever you want and lose the weight. Yes you can lose the weight and get slim but you won't get healthy unless you pay attention to what you're eating.

What's the point in eating less junk food if it's not going to make you healthier just to drop a few dress sizes? Health is about educating yourself and then becoming empowered to take appropriate action.

Transform Your Diet and Feed Your Mind Body and Spirit

I was first introduced to macrobiotics seven years ago when a lady called Judy I had met at one of the many self help seminars I attended, told me she had been following this diet or way of life for a few months after suffering with constant chest pains and high blood pressure. She had reduced her blood pressure to that of a normal healthy person of 120 over 60 from a dangerous 190 over 140. I remember I had been arguing the toss with her about diet and food for some time but I had to admit she looked amazing and the foods seemed to be giving her a real boost. Her skin and eyes were radiant and glowing.

I had grown up pretty much like everyone else, with no previous knowledge of foods and their relation to health; I just ate whatever was put in front of me without a thought as to what and how it would affect my internal organs. As I got older I had read enough books to know my diet was far from great and I also knew I needed to lose some weight but this time for my health rather than vanity. My health had begun to suffer as I was three stone overweight and my high blood pressure was directly related to my weight and eating problems.

Judy persuaded me to try the macrobiotic diet for three months. The deal was that if I didn't find it beneficial or feel any better then she would stop nagging me. The bottom line was I had nothing to lose apart from my weight. So the deal was struck there and then.

The First Few Weeks

The very first few weeks were terrible for me and very boring indeed. I missed my sugary and starchy foods like hell. However as time went on, my enjoyment of the 'new' foods increased and my cravings for my old diet lessened. Within just six weeks I noticed a big improvement in my health and wellness. I was pleasantly surprised when my blood pressure had reduced to almost normal levels and my bowel movements improved, even though I had not been previously aware of any such problem. My energy levels had sky rocketed and I felt a new lease of life come over me as if I had previously lived in a dream like state and now I was awake. I felt light and free, as if something had been holding me down and I had been released from its grip.

The Benefits

By the next time I saw my friend Judy I had been following macrobiotics and read several books on it. Then we both enrolled on a course in making and preparing simple macrobiotic meals to help others, we both decided to create our own unique diet from all the knowledge we had and created 'The Little Genie' diet. We then started arranging small seminars to help others who were looking for an alternative to conventional diets. We were both pleasantly surprised at how well the seminars were received and how quickly they grew from just a couple of people to over a few hundred people at any one time. I had never felt better in my entire life and I had decided to fly to America to meet up with the co-founder of macrobiotics and learn their way of life and the secrets to health and longevity. This is obviously where I learned the most and one of the first things I learned was that macrobiotics was not a diet as we in the west know it, it is a way of life.

Whilst there I realised there was a strong community in Philadelphia for macrobiotics and I met very many people who had overcome serious health problems from cancer, diabetes, asthma, eczema, migraines, cysts, ovarian cancer, heart disease, digestive disorders amongst others. I was able to see firsthand the amazing powers of the macrobiotic diet.

Despite my cynicism about macrobiotics, I continued to experience the health benefits associated with it. Mishio Kushi is recognised as the leading authority in macrobiotics along with the late George Oshawa. If I could give a gift to you now it would be for you to read and learn of this amazing transformation that you can apply to your own life right now. The book I recommend for you to take the first steps into macrobiotics would be "Zen Macrobiotics" by George Oshawa or simply google Macrobiotics under Mishio Kushi the head of the Macrobiotic movement.

What Is 'The Little Genie Diet'?

This is most commonly known as The Ultimate Healing Diet. Macrobiotics is a very flexible and safe way of eating that can help you understand more about which foods are right for you.

Let Food Be Thy Medicine

The food we eat is one of the primary influences on health and because of this The Little Genie Diet focuses on elements of foods that are eaten by some of the world's healthiest societies. In fact, The Little Genie Diet excels in all healthy eating. It is high in fibre, low in fat and has a high mineral content and is high in complex carbohydrates. It uses foods that are essentially low on the glycaemic index. The menus are balanced in sodium and potassium and acid and alkaline. It also has many different cooking styles.

Choose Your Own Style

The Little Genie Diet works on different levels so you could essentially use it to feed yourself more energy, or build a more healthy body, or improve your mind or take greater control of your emotions. You can also do The Little Genie Diet at your own pace - one day at a time or for a short time to see how you feel, just as I did. And eventually you can do it for life. Your choice on the foods you eat goes way beyond eating – you really are what and how you eat. As you will know by now, all living cells are built on the foods you eat and the water you drink and the air you breathe. So it is of paramount importance to know the effects of the foods you eat.

Let's Talk Body Shop

One of the most important reasons for eating The Little Genie Diet is for your body to tell you which foods will be best suited to you. We always tend to shut down the part of us that tells us when we're full. However your body stores a record of all the foods you have eaten in the past and how you eat them and more importantly how your body responds to that food. It knows when you have had sugary foods, how quickly your blood sugar levels rise and that every time you drink coffee you lose fluid and become more acidic. But if you focus a little it is possible to bring this habit to the surface and help you to make the right food choices.

Whole Living Foods

This is extremely important in The Little Genie Diet. Whole foods are still alive up to the point at which they are cooked, and they therefore retain all their goodness and living energy. This living energy interacts with your own life force energy and changes it as a result. This makes you feel different. Whole foods also contain greater nutrients than processed foods which oxidize, losing some of their goodness as a result.

When you start The Little Genie Diet it is most important to experience a whole variety of these whole foods, like brown rice, whole oats and barley, vegetables in season, beans, seeds, nuts and fruits. At least half your food should fall into this category.

Living Energy

George Oshawa and Mishio Kushi developed the link between traditional medicine and macro foods. This built on the idea that everything has a living energy; this is similar to the principles in acupuncture, t'ai chi and yoga. This living energy known as "chi" in China, "ki" in Japan and "prana" in India flows through all living things, including you. This life force energy influences the way we feel and think and affects our health both physically and mentally. Ultimately it impacts most on our health. So in a way similar to the way you might use needles by an acupuncturist or herbs to heal, you can use this powerful healing life force energy in foods to travel deep into your blood and every cell in your body. We all have to eat for as long as we're alive, so why not make each meal you have a healing experience and experience ultimate health.

Changing Your Energy

There are many influences on your energy on a daily basis – the weather, other people, the home you live in, your daily exercise routine but food is one of the most powerful. As already mentioned food has its own living energy and when you eat, you ultimately take it deep inside you, directly changing your own life force energy. The food you eat also changes biological levels and energetic ones. Each meal you eat has the potential to change the way you feel, your emotions and even your long term beliefs and attitude to life.

You have the power to estimate the kind of life force each dish or meal has by looking at the way it grows, its growing season and where it grows, how it is then processed and how it will be cooked. Which means you can actually design a meal to work for you depending on how you want to feel and what will be most beneficial to you.

Example

If you wanted to be more relaxed you might choose a food that is grown in the autumn when the environmental energy is more settled, a food which is round in shape and grows slowly. A sweet taste is more relaxing so again you might choose something like a pumpkin or swede. If you cooked one of these in a stew or soup you would end up with a dish that has slow release energy that spreads throughout the day helping your energy levels to flow throughout the day, You might also use vegetables that grow downwards like carrots or parsnips all with slow release energy.

Yin and Yang. Hot and Cold. Male and Female.

The philosophy of Yin and Yang lies at the heart of Chinese culture. The first references to Yin and Yang come from the 'I Ching', the five classic works compiled and edited by Confucius. Taken literally they mean the dark side and the sunny side of the hill. People most commonly think of Yin and Yang as opposing forces, however, it is more appropriate to think of them as complementary pairs. The Chinese believe that illness and imbalance occur when there is an imbalance of the two. Even divorce or a natural disaster, has been attributed to the imbalance of these forces but how does the concept of Yin and Yang relate to food?

A basic adherence to this philosophy can be found in any Chinese dish, from stir-fried beef with broccoli to sweet and sour pork. There is always a balance in colour, flavours, and textures. However, belief in the importance of following the principles of Yin and Yang in the diet extends further. Certain foods are thought to have Yin or cooling properties, while others have warm, Yang properties. The challenge is to consume a diet that contains a healthy balance between the two. When treating illnesses, an Oriental physician will frequently advise dietary changes in order to restore a healthy balance between the Yin and Yang in the body. For example, let's say you're suffering from heartburn, caused by consuming too many spicy (Yang) foods. Instead of antacids, you're likely to take home a prescription for herbal teas to restore the Yin forces. Similarly, coughs or flu are more likely to be treated with dietary changes than antibiotics or cough medicines.

Cooking Methods:

Yin Method:
- Boiling
- Poaching
- Steaming

Yang Methods:
- Deep Frying
- Roasting
- Stir Frying

Below is a helpful reference to the Yin and Yang theory of foods in The Little Genie Diet, but please make it your business to find out more either by visiting my website or researching the macrobiotic books available through Amazon.

Yin Foods

Cabbage, Bean Sprouts , Carrots , Crab , Cucumber , Duck, Tofu , Water-cress, Water.

Yang Foods

Bamboo , Chicken, Eggs, Ginger, Glutinous Rice, Mushrooms, Sesame Oil, Wine, Beef.

Acid Versus Alkaline

In The Little Genie Diet it is essential to eat living whole foods and some beans and grains. Lentils are acid-forming while vegetables and fruits are alkaline-forming. This is why it is very important to eat as many vegetables and fruits as possible in your daily diet. If you add in fish, or meat or dairy it becomes more acid-forming thus increasing the need for alkaline foods. Eating junk food, smoking or drinking alcohol make the diet even more acid-forming.

Achieving Balance

It is ultimately much easier for the body to balance foods that are closer to nature than to balance out the processed foods that create havoc in your gut and your blood system. It's not quite possible to balance your diet with the two acid-alkaline from a book but you can start to improve your health through making sure you have adequate sources of both.

You can start by having smaller meals. It's easy to put less on your plate than normal and then you could start to introduce equal amounts of grains and vegetables and then try to match equal amounts of acid/alkaline foods.

Example

If you are having fish, reduce your intake of grains slightly and increase your vegetables or fruits. You could try lemon or almonds with your fish. If you like coffee or tea you should also increase more alkaline foods to your diet.

Wonderful Miso

A daily helping of Miso in your daily diet works wonders. Miso is made from fermented soybeans and can be used as a condiment or a drink, it has both cooling and warming properties and has been used in Japan for thousands of years. The many health benefits of Miso have been well documented all over the world. More recently Miso has had a global reputation as a superb and tasty versatile health food; it has been a key ingredient in healthy diets for centuries and does wonders for the body.

Miso for the Elite

Miso was considered a delicacy only eaten by the elite during the 8th and 12th centuries. Nobility and monks would eat it daily but for commoners this wonderfully versatile healthy food was out of bounds. It was also given in exchange for wages to society's elite rather than used as a condiment. During this period Miso would normally have been eaten straight or spread on food directly.

Eat Miso soup every day for better health

Miso soup can help gastric disorders. Studies have shown that people who regularly have Miso soup cut their chances of Gastric Cancer and stomach disorders, such as Gastritis, Gastric Ulcers or Duodenal Ulcers. Miso is rich in digestive enzymes and provides protection for the stomach lining. Studies have also shown that Miso helps to prevent Breast Cancer and the aging process through the anti-oxidant properties found in Miso.

There are simply so many health benefits to this wonder food that I cannot mention all of them in this book but I do encourage you to research for yourself. In the meantime you can buy it from online health foods shops and certain supermarkets and you can use it as a drink by adding one teaspoon to a cup of hot boiling water.

Diakon

The Giant Radish for Health

Diakon is a giant white radish or, as it is most commonly known in the west under its Indian name, Mooli. Diakon means great root in Japanese, which is very appropriate as it is shaped like a carrot but much bigger in size. Diakon has a very distinct flavour a bit like horseradish, but smoother and milder.

Diakon a delicious source of Vitamin C, calcium and iron; it is also known as a specific aid in the digestion of oily foods. It has been shown that the enzymes contained in the vegetable, such as diastase, help to dissolve accumulated fat and mucus deposits. It is little wonder, then, that it is so often found alongside oily foods when they occur in the Japanese diet and has been an integral part of Japanese folk medicine for so long.

If you suffer from heart disease or high cholesterol then eating diakon with other healthy foods will help to reduce or completely eliminate the fatty deposits from your arteries increase your vitality and prolong your life.

How to Cook With Dried Diakon

To reconstitute, soak in lukewarm water for about 30-45 minutes. Remove and squeeze out the excess water. You can use this water for stock, sauté alone or with other vegetables and season to taste. You can also use it in hearty winter soups or stews.

The Potent Umboshi Plum

Umboshi plums are one of Japan's most remarkable traditional foods, revered from ancient times as both a potent health tonic and an everyday food.

The umboshi pickled plum has a very sharp distinct taste and a zesty, cleansing flavour with fast acting medicinal effects.

Even today some Japanese people start their day with two umboshi plums and a cup of Mugi tea or other traditional Japanese tea. The very tarty, tangy taste will make your hairs stand on end from the moment you first taste it. You always remember the first time you taste this magical super food. Japanese pickled plums have a remarkable alkalizing effect on the body, neutralising fatigue, stimulating digestion and promoting the elimination of mouth ulcers. It's like sandpaper on your taste-buds but will rid your body of toxins. This is, in my opinion, the equivalent to both Aspirin for the thining of your blood and apples for their vitamins.

Although particularly effective for all sorts of stomach disorders from hyper-acidity and indigestion to ulcers, umboshi also increases endurance and stimulates the liver and kidney functions of dissolving and expelling toxins, thus purifying the blood. As every Japanese housewife learns at an early age, umboshi's powerful anti-bacterial properties make it very effective in preventing rice from spoiling. Ancient medical texts also credit umboshi with preventing food poisoning. Umboshi's alkalinizing effect makes it a wonderful general tonic. Added to "soft rice" (rice cooked 7-10:1 with water until very soft), umboshi is the Japanese cure-all for sick children.

Like many of Japan's ancient medicinal foods, the origin of the pickled plum is obscure. One theory traces it to China, where a dried smoked plum, or ubai, was discovered in a tomb built over two thousand years ago. The "ubai" is one of China's oldest medicines and is still used for a variety of medical purposes such as counteracting nausea, reducing fevers, and controlling coughs.

One of the oldest Japanese stories records pickled plums being used as a medicine in a textbook written about one thousand years ago. Umboshi were used to prevent fatigue, purify water, rid the body of toxins and cure specific diseases such as dysentery, typhoid and food poisoning. Slowly, extensive folklore developed about umboshi's ability to prevent and cure certain diseases.

During Japan's samurai period, which lasted through most of the Middle Ages, the pickled plum was the soldier's most important field ration. It was used to flavour foods such as rice and vegetables and its high acidity made it an excellent water and food purifier, as well as an effective antidote for battle fatigue.

Sea Vegetables

Although the thought of eating sea vegetables may seem strange at first, these wonder foods from the ocean are super healthy and all our ancestors would have had them as part of a staple diet. Their high concentration of minerals is close to that of minerals in human blood. Specifically, sea vegetables contain high amounts of calcium phosphorous, magnesium, sodium, iron and iodine. Sea vegetables are chelating agents which mean they have the ability to remove heavy metals from the body. Sea vegetables are also a wonderful source of photo-chemicals. Sea vegetables can also have a balancing affect on the thyroid which can have a positive impact on many health related issues. Because of this, sea vegetables should be considered as part of your daily diet for health and longevity.

Here is a list of the most commonly used sea vegetables

- **Wakame**

Is a sea vegetable that needs soaking and can be used in soups. Soak for about ten minutes until it doubles in size then drain off any excess water and add to soups.

- **Arame**

Does not need cooking but does need to be soaked before you eat it for about fifteen minutes and is a great compliment to garden fresh salad.

- **Dulse**

Can be bought as flakes and added to your salad or salad dressing giving a touch of salt to the flavour, especially liked by children.

- **Hijiki**

Hijiki' was given the name "Beauty Vegetable " by the Japanese as it is said to give women their lustrous long hair and beautiful skin, again this needs to be soaked for about fifteen minutes and you can serve it with vegetables and fish.

- **Kombu**

Kombu can be added to soups and gives a nice salty flavour and will soften as it cooks. There is no need to add any salt to meals when using sea vegetables as they carry enough already.

113

- **Irish Moss '**

Can be used as a thickening agent to any liquid, simply add to the soup or liquid and allow cooling.

- **Nori'**

Nori is probably the most widely known of sea vegetables as it is used to make sushi and that is exactly what you can do with this very versatile sea vegetable.

- **Agar Agar**

Agar Agar is wonderful when used as a thickening agent for puddings and gelatines a very healthy addition to any food that needs to be thickened.

Sea vegetables are indeed a super food and should be used at least three times a week if not daily, once you start to add these super foods to your daily diet you will begin to notice significant health changes.

Like everything else, I can only tell you what I know to be facts and I am in no way a medical doctor nor do I wish to be one. If you have a medical condition it is up to you to seek proper medical advice and I encourage you to do so.

I just want to open up your mind and hope you will seek further information on the food and health topics mentioned above. One thing I do know is that if you eat all the foods mentioned above your health will greatly improve and hopefully you will find the strength within you to pursue this quest for a better healthier life and find your freedom.

Things You Will Need:

✓ Miso
✓ Umboshi Plums
✓ Diakon Radish

- ✓ Tofu
- ✓ Sea Vegetables
- ✓ Fresh Fruits and Vegetables
- ✓ Nuts And Seeds
- ✓ Pulses
- ✓ Green Tea/Japanese Kuchi Tea

Places you can find most of the foods mentioned in this book including places of interest and books of interest

www.amozen.co.uk

Zen Macrobiotics and other books Macrobiotic books can be found here.

www.michiokushi.org

www.kushiinstitute.org

www.macrobiotics.co.uk

Macrobiotic Food Stores

www.clearspring.co.uk

www.goodnessdirect.co.uk

www.naturalgrocery.co.uk

www.planetorganic.co.uk

Supermarkets

Morrisons - In Health Food Section

Sainsburys - In the Wellbeing and Special Selections

Tesco - In the Speciality Food fixture

Waitrose - Sushi & miso ranges, fruit purees, Japanese teas

Your Body Never Lies

Your body is constantly giving off signals. If you feel sluggish after eating a meal then you have eaten poorly. If you feel alive and energetic then you have eaten a meal high in energy for you.

Remember to eat your food slowly and chew each mouthful at least 30-60 times, the more you chew the better you will feel and the easier it will be for your body to digest.

All these foods can be found in health foods shops online under macrobiotic foods - my favourite place is clearspring.

Eat all of these foods daily and chew your food in combination with fresh fruits and vegetables and your health and vitality will increase daily.

"Let Food be thy medicine and medicine be thy food"

15

The Laughter Effect

Research has shown that happy people are usually healthy people. That is why it is of great importance to be able to laugh and not take things too seriously. A good sense of humour is your key to great happiness. Think of it as essential in your psychological profile. When you laugh and feel good your body gives off different chemical reactions.

You can often use this mind-set to alleviate pain and discomfort. It's a known fact that when you are laughing or smiling you feel less pain. Laughter is more infectious than a cough or a sneeze. When laughter is shared with someone else it binds people together and breaks down barriers and increases happiness and intimacy.

Laughter Is A Strong Medicine

Laughter is a powerful antidote to pain. Nothing works better or faster to bring your mind and body back in to harmony. All humour will lighten and inspire you towards better things and you feel more focused and alert.

It has the power to heal and renew your very own living cells, enhancing your physical and emotional health.

Start Now With Yourself

Practise these inner-smiling techniques anytime anywhere.

1. Sit comfortably in a chair or lie down.
2. Allow a smile to cross your lips.
3. Smile into a part of your body that feels neglected until it begins to loosen up and relax.
4. Now smile into all other parts of your body - all your internal organs and express great gratitude for them.
5. Smile at the brain and imagine it telling yourself 'I Love You'.
6. Smile into your past and thank it for being there and all you have learned.
7. Finally smile into your future and imagine all the wonderful things you're about to experience in this new future you.
8. Take a few moments now to really imagine and visualise this wonderful new life, then come back out.

You have to be smiling now even if you weren't before. Try to keep smiling each new day and see the difference as things start to take on a new meaning.

16

Believe In Yourself

We all have beliefs about different things. But what is interesting is whenever I'm with a new client and I ask them why they believe a certain thing, they always answer 'I don't know' or 'I'm not sure'. In effect what they really mean is: it's all unconscious and they don't know where the belief really came from because it was probably instilled into them as they grew up through parents, family and friends.

The good news is beliefs are neither the truth nor a lie they are just beliefs, usually learnt through a person's judgement of how they were brought up. And the other good news is we can change any unhelpful beliefs at anytime. We can in effect build a whole new belief system that is more in line with who we are; a new belief system that fits with our goals and values.

When you were little you depended on your parents to teach you and help you make sense of the world. As you grew up, you were filled with your parents beliefs about how you should behave and how other people should behave back, you were also taught how to believe in the same things they do through constant repetition throughout the years.

Example

When you did something that your parents didn't approve of you would have been punished, I know for me it was always early to bed and a good telling off. So this would send a message constantly to my brain that this kind of behaviour wasn't acceptable and if I wanted to be liked more or loved more I should change my behaviour to that which is in keeping with my parent's beliefs. Trouble with that was I didn't know all my parents beliefs because I was just a kid. So I only knew of their disapproval once I had not pleased them with my own actions or beliefs.

Then when I had grown up I brought with me all my parents beliefs about myself: the world we live in and how other people should behave - not thinking for one moment they could be wrong or totally out of character to who I really am. Why? Because I trusted them, they were my parents and after all, most parents want the best for their children.

If you're a parent you can start to recognise your own behaviour now with your children and help to build better relations with them through learning a few simple unconscious communication techniques that will give you and your children the greatest gift of all - freedom.

Notice Your Language and How You Use It

Did you know that 80% of communication is made through non-verbal means? Tone and pitch of voice, body language, hand gestures and eye contact (or lack of it) are just a few of the ways we communicate without words. Sometimes we forget that, despite our children being younger than we are, they are still impacted by this non-verbal language. Try to spend a few minutes noticing what type of communication you are giving to your child non-verbally.

Many have said that how you say something is much more

important than what you say. That could not be a more accurate statement than when it comes to impressionable young minds. Children as young as 18 months old are attuned not only to your voice but also to your body language. If you whisper when they are screaming, they are more likely to stop screaming because they want to hear what you are saying. When your child is whining that he wants sweets or a toy, how do you respond? If you huff and growl and complain back as you roll your eyes, your child hears, 'You are not good enough for me to take the time to properly deal with you.' However, if you kneel down on their level and calmly explain why they are not getting the thing they want, they are getting the message, 'You are very important to me and I want to make sure I take care of you.' In this instance alone, you can see that body language sends a far more powerful message than words alone.

There are many different messages you can send to your child with your body. An easy example of this is where you look when you talk to them. If you look into their eyes and talk, your message is more likely to stay in their brain. If you yell at him from across the house, they will probably not pay any attention.

Experts offer various opinions about the best ways to communicate with others. There are theories about what and how you should speak and how you should not speak. If you tend to argue a lot, make sure you don't argue with, or in front of, your children. Your children need a steady hand and a steady voice at all times.

You may think, 'My child spends most of their time at school and with friends; is it still that important that I learn how to communicate with them?' The answer is a resounding, yes! Your child will spend more time with you than with any other adult - probably even their teacher - and as their parent, you will control to some extent who their friends are and who they spend their time with. You will be their most influential teacher in their early years and if you develop good communication skills with your children now, it will set the pattern for a healthy relationship for their entire lives.

Your Own Parents and Their Communication Techniques

Remember your experiences communicating with your parents and siblings during the years when you were growing up? Often, we emulate our parents' techniques once we become parents ourselves.

We have all usually had our fair share of rivalry with our siblings and have memories of our parents breaking us up from one fight or another. Whenever it came time to discipline, many parents would use very different techniques to get their message across. For example, your dad may have told you to do something once and if you did not obey, he may not have repeated his request or yelled. He may have sent you to your room, which is a good way of getting your child out of a situation where you may be tempted to yell at them. He may then have come upstairs after a few minutes (after he had time to cool off) and perhaps taken a favourite toy away as a punishment for your behaviour. This is a good time to talk to your child about what they have done and how next time they could do better.

Your Mum, on the other hand, may have used a different

technique. She may have told you to do something once. If you did not obey, she may have looked at you and raised her eyebrows as a reminder. If you still did not obey, she may have said your name with a warning tone in her voice. Then she may have sent you to your room and come in and talk to you about why you disobeyed her. She might have made sure you understood that you had done wrong and needed discipline. Talking to your kids about what they have done wrong and why it is wrong is very important, since it helps them understand and do better next time. By being consistent with discipline, parents can anchor in their child's mind the link between disobedience and punishments such as grounding. With time, such parenting tactics can help your child to replace his bad behaviour with good obedience, respect, and trustworthiness.

There may have been times when your parents had been at work all day long and you may not have seen them very much during the day. The times that you did spend together may still be filled with very good memories; however, this may be largely down to the way your parents communicated with you. Parents can use not just words but also body language very effectively to let their children know that they love them and want only the best for them.

When you talk to your child, be sure to maintain eye contact, touch them and smile and nod when your child is talking to you. Whenever your child comes to you asking for advice, always ask them first what they think they should do, but do it in a way that lets them know you care but want them to think for themselves.

If you home school your children, you probably get to

spend a lot of time with them every day. There are probably many times when your kids may have a problem, either with studies or with their siblings, and as a parent you would do well to encourage them to think creatively to find a solution. You should not avoid talking to your children because you are too busy to help them; on the contrary, you should always take the time to talk to your children about different things that are of interest to them. If the problem is too great for them to solve on their own, or if all their solutions do not resolve the problem, offer a suggestion with an encouraging smile. No matter how busy you are, always take the time to find out if anything is bothering your child.

The strong foundation of communication laid when you are a child helps you as an adult and can also help you to determine your own parenting style. In order to maintain a healthy relationship with your children through their lives, you need to use good communication skills with them when they are young.

Believing Yourself Healthy

A few years ago a lot of research was going on to try and discover why a small number of people survived cancer while the majority do not survive. The study revealed that around a hundred people who had been diagnosed with terminal cancer were still alive around twelve years after.

The research was originally to study any differences in the patterns of thinking and behaviour of these hundred patients. The results were quite amazing but conclusive. They had all used different treatments, varying from surgery to acupuncture to natural diets, some even did psychological techniques, but all one hundred people shared the same thought:

They believed they would recover and be well and what they were doing would work for them.

I used the same thought patterns about myself when I first started writing, I believed I was good enough and that I could learn to write just as well as anyone else, if not better; even though I had no previous experience or qualifications, I just knew I could do it.

In medical history there is an interesting demonstration about the power of beliefs known as the placebo effect. A placebo is a tablet with no content so to speak, it doesn't do anything for you, it simply has nothing in it. Because the United States require all new drugs to be tested against placebos, there is a lot more research on them than normal.

On average placebos are about 30 per cent as effective as a medical drug. However, in some specific cases their effectiveness is much higher. Compared against morphine, placebos are 54 per cent as effective, even though morphine is a class 'A' drug. We as human beings are only just beginning to understand the power of our brains and how hypnosis plays a big role in medicine and surgery. Some doctors are already using the power of hypnosis in their practice including heart surgeons and GPs.

People who believe they can control their immune system find they can easily do so by using techniques like self-hypnosis or guided imagery techniques. This will instantly improve their resistance to illnesses.

It's amazing What You Can Do

When You Don't Know That You Can't

In 1952 Dr. Albert Mason was treating a fifteen year old boy for warts using hypnosis. Dr. Mason amongst other doctors had previously used hypnosis to cure warts but this time he faced an even greater challenge. Except for the skin on the boy's chest he was covered in warts.

Dr. Mason concentrated on the boy's arm. While the boy was in a trance, he suggested that his skin on that arm would heal and turn pink and healthy.

When Dr. Mason brought the boy to the referring surgeon, who had unsuccessfully tried to help the boy with skin grafts; he learned that he had made a medical error. The surgeon's eyes were wide with astonishment when he saw the boy's arm. He told Dr. Mason that he was suffering, not from warts but from a lethal genetic disease called congenital ichthyosis. By reversing the symptoms using only the power of the mind, Dr. Mason and the boy accomplished what was until then deemed impossible.

Dr. Mason continued with his hypnosis sessions with the boy and the amazing results showed when his arm looked like the healthy, pink arm after the first hypnosis session. The boy, who had been bullied in school because of his grotesque-looking skin, went on to lead a perfectly normal life.

When Dr. Mason wrote about his wonderful treatment in the British Medical Journal in 1952, his article created a sensation. He became very popular for people suffering with this rare disease that up until then had been deemed incurable.

Boost Your Own Immune System

Your immune system is nothing short of miraculous, with healing powers you could never imagine. The powers can be enhanced even more through some very simple visualization techniques I'm going to share with you now. Here's an example of the powers of the same visualization techniques.

1. Close your eyes and imagine your immune system by giving it a colour, preferably a calming colour that you like. Make sure you see this as a strong and powerful immune system.
2. Now, imagine a white beam of light has travelled through the top of your head and down into your body, to the area around your immune system.
3. Now you notice the white beam of healing light touch upon the immune system and destroy any black cells that are not working correctly.
4. Now that the white healing beam of light has destroyed the black cells it's very important to imagine the good cells that you originally

   gave a colour to floating about strong and powerful protecting your blood system.
5. Now imagine a healthier you standing in front of yourself. See how this new healthier you looks, feels and smiles.
6. Now finally, step into the new healthier you and feel all the good feelings as you get used to this healthier new you.

You can automatically turn on this white healing power whenever you feel down or ill for whatever reason. Remember its power – just as you would switch on a light and at the flick of the switch a white beam of light shines, so can you. You can do this in any situation from curing yourself from all kinds of diseases. I've even known cancer patients try this miraculous switch with very positive results.

17

Your Right to Be Rich

You cannot become rich by thinking small so, as we have already discussed throughout this book, you need to change your mindset to acquire the wealth you so rightly deserve. Whenever I hear people praise poverty it sends shivers down my spine because you do not serve the world by being small. No one can reach their true potential by being poor.

To show your true talent and soul, you must have many things, and to get those things you have to have money with which to buy them. The true object in life is to develop and continually learn so that you can reach you highest potential physically, mentally and spiritually. All human beings have this right to reach the highest development possible.

When I hear people say 'oh that will do' it makes me cringe. No one should ever be satisfied with so little if they are capable of enjoying and having more. And we are capable of so much more. The full purpose of all nature is to unfold its greatness day by day including its beauty, richness, and elegance. To be content with anything less is a sin.

Any man or women who is living abundantly with all the resources he or she has available to them is rich. And equally any man or women who hasn't reached their true potential can have all he or she wants. Life is now so advanced that we each need vast amounts of money to become complete. People usually have high hopes of great wealth and happiness, we all desire to become more and this is a good thing. But then we lose sight of the game and as soon as we see something a little too far out of our reach, we switch back to being comfortable.

Let me tell you something that I hope you will remember throughout this book. There is nothing wrong with wanting to get rich. That desire is actually the desire to be happier, and that desire is very praiseworthy. Anyone who does not desire the riches to buy all they want is abnormal.

We live for our mind, body, and soul, neither or any of these is less important than the other and so if one or all of these are not working properly or to their optimum then we are neither full nor complete. It is not good to only live for a part of our whole selves, meaning if you only live your life to feed your soul without feeding the mind and body you can never be fully complete.

You can see an expression of this in everyday life, whenever I hear a woman say I need to lose weight, what she means is I need to lose this fat from my body in order be more happy or more complete but then when she loses the weight she is much happier but she still feels there is something missing (Body Richness) then after closer scrutiny she discovers she is not happy with her partner (Mind Richness) and her beliefs about what she can achieve (Soul Richness). We have all experienced these feelings at some point in our lives, yet still put up with less.

Man cannot live fully in body without good food, clothing, and shelter and without freedom from excessive problems. Plenty of rest and friendships are also necessary to one's physical life. One cannot live fully in the mind without study of books, travel, observation and intellectual companions. To read and study books is to reach your true potential because knowledge is power. You should also have the things around you that will inspire you: such as beautiful paintings or furniture. To live fully in soul, man most also have love; and love is denied expression by poverty.

Love finds its natural expression of love through giving. A man who has nothing to give cannot fill his place in this great big universe, the natural cycle of life is to give and receive. When you give wholeheartedly you will receive more than you can ever imagine. And I don't just mean giving money or gifts; I mean giving yourself, your love, your fortune, your knowledge, your time, all of these things are giving.

There is a way of getting rich, an exact way, but there are certain rules to getting rich which must be learned and obeyed. Once you have learned and obeyed them you will, with mathematical certainty, become rich.

Discovering the Secrets to Wealth

To become rich one must do certain things in a certain way; and those who do those things in a certain way, whether on purpose or accidentally, will get rich; while those who do not do things in a certain way, even if they work hard, will remain poor. It is a universal law that determines whether your life will be rich or poor.

Getting rich isn't about where you live, because if it was only people in certain neighbourhoods who become wealthy; people from one city would be rich, while those from other cities would be poor. Getting rich is nothing to do with environment. But we can see evidence of both rich and poor living side-by-side in the same cities and environment usually engaged in the same kind of things. When men and women are in the same location and doing the same job and one gets rich while the other stays poor, it is usually an indication that getting rich is a result of doing things in a certain way.

To become rich it is not necessary to be talented. Many people who have great talent remain poor, while some people who have no talent get rich. When I studied the people who had got rich, I discovered they had similarities but had no greater talents or abilities than ordinary men or women. They just happen to do things in a certain way. And acquiring wealth has little to do with saving money or being careful with it.

If like causes produce like effects, then anyone who follows a few simple rules can become rich - this is an exact science. You would be entitled to ask 'is this certain way so difficult that only a select few can follow it?' The truth is, very talented people get rich and a total fool can also get rich; just as weak people can get rich and strong people can get rich. It is of course essential that one has the ability to at least think and understand but the fact remains any man or woman who can think and act, or who can read and understand this book can get rich. Also, as we have discovered, it has nothing to do with environment but location does count for something - one would not go to the desert to do business: to get rich you need to be near other people and if these people are inclined to deal with you in your way so much the better, other than that you can be successful wherever you are.

If you see people in your town who are rich, you may envy them. But it is within your gift to earn as much as them. Similarly, if you see someone who is famous, you can be famous too. And it's not about a particular business or profession. People get rich from every kind of profession and in every business; while someone in the same vocation in the same street or town can be skint. But it is true that you will do best in a business you actually like. Likewise you will do best in a business suited to your locality; a shop selling air conditioning would do well in a warmer climate than a colder one for example.

So apart from these few limitations, getting rich is not dependent on you engaging in some particular business model but upon you learning to do things in a certain way. If you are in business at this moment and someone else in your locality is in the same business and they are getting rich while you are not, it is because you are not doing things in the same way he or she is doing them. No one is preventing you from getting rich through lack of capital. It is true, as your capital increases business becomes easier but by then you will already be rich...

No matter how poor you may be, if you start to do things in a certain way you will get rich and you will have capital. Getting capital is all part and parcel of getting rich. You could be the poorest person on the planet and be deep in debt. You may not have friends or resources but if you start to do things in a certain way you will get rich. If you are in the wrong kind of business you should get in the right kind of business; if you have no capital you can get capital; if you are in the wrong location you should move to the right location.

Opportunities

There isn't a man or women who has to be poor because opportunity has been taken away from them because others have monopolized the wealth and put up a fence. You may be shut off from certain businesses but there are other channels. Of course it would be difficult to get control of any of the big supermarket chains; but there are plenty of opportunities for online supermarkets, especially those who specialize in a particular product. The working class can become the elite class when they learn to master things in a certain way; the law of wealth is no different for them as it is for others.

No one is kept in poverty through a short supply because there is more than enough for everyone; in fact the pot just keeps getting bigger. The visual supply is practically inexhaustible and the invisible supply really is inexhaustible.

Everything you see has been borne of a thought and substance, out of which everything else proceeds. New forms are constantly being made and out of date or older ones are being dissolved. Nature is an endless storehouse of riches.

Overcome Poverty Consciousness

Research has shown that some people, who get rich by accident, from lottery wins or an inheritance, usually end up losing all their money two or three years later. Why? Because inside they still feel poor. This is better known to you and me as "a self-fulfilling prophecy" what we expect to be true in our minds usually has a way of becoming just so and usually, because we are continually thinking those thoughts on a daily basis, they come true.

If you really believe you cannot get rich then the chances are you won't but if you change your thinking to that of infinite wealth and richness and believe you deserve these riches then the chances are you will get rich.

You can take full responsibility for your beliefs and actions (including your wealth consciousness) right now. However if you are poor it is not your fault. We are not responsible for the hand we are dealt but we must take full responsibility in how we play that hand; that is the difference.

Example

Some people stay poor because it feels safe. It's what they know; or some people often think or believe that you cannot be a truly good person unless you are always putting other people first.

As you go through this system with me you will learn to let go of all these self-limiting beliefs about money and success. You can start by reprogramming your mind for abundant wealth and have a millionaire mindset. Here are two mental laws that show the differences between the rich and poor mindset.

'Whatever you resist will persist'

Some people have very deep rooted beliefs that keep them in poverty. It seems that no matter how hard these people try to get rich consciously; their unconscious beliefs do not support them. This is when you need to have a good dose of hypnosis or self-hypnosis, which you can perform on your own in your own time. By doing this you will collapse the old operating software in your subconscious mind that will help you reach your new potential.

Of course it's not enough to just delete the old operating software you also need to put something back in there to fill the empty space. This is where you will put your new beliefs about yourself and your desires for a better life. Such as saying to yourself 'every day in every way I get better and better in every way' or another phrase you find appropriate for what you want out of life - make sure to include everything and keep adding new phrases on a daily basis.

If you focus your attention on poverty that is exactly what you will get from life. If, however, you focus on wealth and riches that are already available to you in your unconscious mind, that is what you will get. Think of it this way - do you know someone who is naturally positive and no matter what anyone says they always see the positives instead of the negatives. These kinds of people are usually thought to be "The Lucky Ones" and whilst there are naturally lucky people I personally believe we can make our own luck in life. That's exactly what the bible says "so a man thinketh he becomes". Of course it's entirely up to you whether you believe in the laws of attraction or not, but most highly successful people do. This is also why most very rich people associate with other very rich people and get even richer.

People often attract the kind of people into their lives who they think they deserve to be around. So if you are attracting the wrong type of person then it's highly likely that your unconscious has some work to do in order for you to start attracting more positive and wealthy people.

If you want riches and the life that goes with it; you must start today to see yourself as the kind of person who deserves to have all these riches and that it is your birth right to have everything your heart desires. A good way to do this is to think rich from the inside so it manifests itself outwardly.

The universe desires you to have everything you want, nature is extremely friendly to your plans of a better life and you must make this sentence uppermost in your conscious and unconscious mind.

So when you are doing self-hypnosis later on today, I want you to repeat the sentence above several times until you firmly belief it to be so. Then repeat it each and every day. It's like magic. Watch as all you desires begin to unfold.

18

Clear Your Mind, Prepare To Shine

Changing your self-image will help you develop a wealth consciousness; this will help you have big doses of confidence and harmony in your everyday life. You can create now in your mind the exact thing which you so desire.

People often think daydreaming is a waste of time. Personally I see it as a great resource to future riches when it is used to one's advantage. What I mean is purposely daydream your new life and see how your life changes to one of wealth, health and complete happiness.

I remember when I was younger and just starting to learn all this stuff, I was constantly worried about money and afraid of being poor – so guess what I attracted? I had no money and was poor until I realised what I was doing; I immediately changed my mind set and decided I had nothing to lose by thinking of myself as already rich – all that was left to do was manifest the money and the lifestyle to go with it. I started to visualise myself as the person I wanted to be and the car I wanted to drive and the house of my dreams. When I started to do this, two things changed dramatically. I started to get more phone calls for my business and I was invited to a celebrity party. I realised this stuff was actually working when my contact list for business kept growing daily - it was as if I could feel it, smell it, almost reach out and touch it, I knew it was there just waiting for me.

As I continued on this same line of thinking (consciously and unconsciously) my life changed completely within two short years, things happened just out of the blue, I suddenly had the opportunity to write a book including this one. I had also met up with a friend from years ago who I had lost contact with who just become a first time author.

I also made a wealth scrap book and to my surprise at least three things in my scrap book have become a reality. I'm still working on my final successes but I know it's going to happen - it's just a matter of time.

My scrap book has pictures of things I want, like a car, house, bank balance, places I want to visit, people I want to meet and so forth. I just keep adding to it every day or every time I see something new that I want.

You too can create your own scrap book and anything you want to bring into your life add it to your scrap book. Then you can start daydreaming about each thing in your scrap book.

Example

If you have a particular house in your scrap book that you want to own, you might start thinking about the house as you relax and drift into a relaxed hypnotic state, then try to imagine you're inside the house, see it in full colour, visualise the rooms one by one as you walk through it. Visualise what you would like to have in each room until you have filled all the rooms in the house with your own personal furniture and belongings. Alternatively see the car or cars you want parked up outside or in the drive, now all you have to do is make sure you are fully associated with the picture and images in your mind and you are not a bystander.

You can use this technique for each of the things you want to attract into your life one at a time, try to visualise them on a daily basis; the more you do this, the quicker you will get them. You have to believe it is already yours and that you deserve it.

Real Wealth

Of course, real wealth isn't just about material things and money – it's about the access to wealth that all of us have available to us. Think about all that you have available to you even if you have no money. You have access to resources that can make you money.

Real wealth is also about having good health, true happiness and good friends and family who can share all these wonderful experiences with love and laughter. Remember money is just a translator of how well you have done in this life. And in the kind of world we now live in its good to have plenty of it so that you can live life as you truly want it and experience living to the fullest extent. Now for the tricky bit – if you want to be rich beyond imagination you have work to do. And that work evolves you having the right attitude and complete belief in your own worth.

It's certainly not enough to just provide a service or goods in exchange for riches. The more confidence in yourself and your product or service, the more we can charge in real money.

Once you own this confidence you will own the riches. You have everything it could possibly take to become rich.

No matter what social status you belong to, no one is barred from attaining wealth, in fact it's your birth right. No man or women is incapable of growing. Yes it's true we are born with unconscious tendencies, as for instance a tendency to be shy or bad tempered, but all these can be overcome. You can rid yourself of these unhelpful subconscious tendencies and replace them with more desirable ones that help to support your new goals for a wealthy life. Think of yourself as rich and you will be. Think of yourself as poor and that's exactly what you'll remain.

Anchoring Wealth

Think of all the feelings having more money will bring to your life. This might be confidence, happiness or being more generous. Choose the first one you thought about and do the following exercise.

1. Think of a time when you felt utterly confident and now fully return to it. See what you saw, hear what you heard and feel all the good feelings associated with it.
2. Keep going through the visualization process and make the images bigger, brighter and louder.
3. When you are fully associated and feeling confident, squeeze your thumb and finger on your right hand together and repeat these words out loud. 'I am Rich'. Repeat it at least five times until you feel you really are already rich.
4. Keep repeating each one on your list with the same technique, repeating 'I am rich', this is like your richness anchor for success, so use it anytime you want to attract more richness and wealth into

your life.

Health and Wealth and Happiness Combined

There are some people in the world who have more health than wealth and some people with more wealth than health... and that may not make them very happy. But imagine now if you could have both; in fact you might just be a person who already has both which is great news because you might just find yourself living longer and better than anyone who doesn't have both health and wealth.

Don't Sacrifice One for the Other

Many people I have met sacrifice one for the other but in my opinion if you sacrifice your health over wealth this would surely be very foolish because if you are dead then wealth doesn't really matter because you're not here to enjoy the wealth. We all know people who are working hard in a job they hate but keep doing it for the money, never thinking they could be working at something they love.

Prioritize

Of all the three above, in my own opinion health has to be a number one priority over wealth and happiness because without it you can't be happy or truly wealthy. So if you are sacrificing your health over happiness then you need to start thinking more about how much longer you will keep on doing the things that keep you poor and unhappy. If you're not doing what you love then start today. Follow your dream and keep going no matter what. You will reach your goals much quicker than doing something you hate just for the money.

Start investing in things you love. Some of you have probably heard the saying to work at the things you love. This is true but too many people invest in things they don't know a lot about, things they are not particularly interested in and do not love. I only ever invest in things I love. I love reading and writing and I love people so I know I'm more likely to study hard the things which I love. Not only will I study them more but I will be more likely to succeed in any of these things.

I can remember taking some photos to be developed from a holiday in California with my husband. When I looked at them I saw one in particular that stood out like a sore thumb. I thought I looked really fat. Looking at it shocked me so much that I immediately started to look at my health more seriously. It wasn't the fact that I was overweight which shocked me it was thinking of spending less time with my husband and family that shocked me into taking action. I decided to invest in my own health that day and never looked back. By doing this I got two things – better health and much more happiness. Remember: to invest in yourself is to invest in your future.

Spend a day and think about your life and your desires to succeed at the things you love the most. Think about the ways in which you can follow your dreams instead of thinking of ways you can't. This is your life here and now, there is no other time for you to make your life great. This is your only chance to be everything you ever wanted to be. Be bold and start today.

"Lack of money is the root of all evil"
GEORGE BERNARD SHAW

19

The Intelligence of Thinking

If you want to be great at anything you have to have great thoughts. If you only have greatness outside and not on the inside then you are not great. There is no amount of education or reading that can make you great without thought. There are a lot of people who try to make something great about themselves through reading and education but fail to really think about what they read. You cannot develop mentally by what you read only by what you think you read.

I have met many people who think they are great at something. We all know someone who thinks they are great at something and when you find out they are not it's pretty disappointing to all their hard work go down the plughole. After all, if they have been to university and done, say, a degree in medicine, they may have all the text book learning and know how to save your life in an emergency or take blood from your arm or even how to recognise symptoms of illness but it hasn't taught them how to engage a personality. I remember a doctor once who told me he knew more than I did about my own body - how absurd is that! He wasn't prepared to listen to my opinion, even though it was my body that I had lived in for the previous thirty-four years. Some doctors don't like to think you know more about your body than they do and find it quite upsetting when you can point out the obvious. I'm not saying they aren't good at saving lives but you have the resources inside you to know what your body is telling you, if only you listen.

Your body has a greater intelligence than anything on earth. Your body never lies. According to how we feel at any one moment, your body will tell you what's wrong and we can usually tell from our own instincts how to fix it or make it better. We have lost the ancient art of listening to our bodies. It is only now in this very busy, fast-paced world in which we live that society and government has taught us to rely on conventional medicine to heal our bodies when they become sick.

The Truth about Food and Drugs

Unfortunately, unless we go back to these old traditional healing arts we may never experience true health, each time we take conventional medicine we weaken the body and its ability to fight off illness. Think of this - the pharmaceutical industry is a business and like any business it has to have customers, the more customers it gets the bigger and richer it becomes. They don't want to have healthy people walking the planet and taking their health into their own hands because that would mean the end of business for them. So they have to keep you sick by having more drugs to counteract the first one and so on, you get what I mean here it's a downward spiral that has got out of control in my opinion. Now they even want you to believe that alternative cures are all hocus ocus' especially hypnosis. Why? Because if we all knew how powerful hypnosis and other alternative methods really were then no-one would need so many of their drugs.

Then there are the supermarket chains who sell foods that would kill you if you were to carry on eating them. I remember a newspaper I picked up recently had an article that caught my eye on a certain well known fast food restaurant whose burgers had been left in a room for a whole year as part of an experiment to see how they would decompose. Unfortunately the burger wasn't even good enough for the birds and bees. After a whole year went by the burger was shown to be almost the same as the day it was left, proving how much of it was preservative and hydrogenated fats. Can you imagine what that does to your insides when you eat it?

Just like fast food chains, supermarkets word their products and ingredients very cleverly so most average people wouldn't know what was in their food. You have to take back control of your health now before it's too late and for your children's sake as much as your own. There are many business interests that would prefer you remained ignorant. By taking control of your health and happiness you are stopping them from earning big profits off the misery of you and your family. So please, take action now and take control of your own body – no one knows what's right for you more than you. You have the ultimate power over your well being.

Think of all the richness and health your body and mind can experience when you give up take away and fast food and replace it with natural home cooked foods. Life can be great when you go back to the simple things and heal your mind and body through eating for health rather than convenience.

Remember To Eat Healthily

When you eat the foods mentioned in this book you can improve your life and well being. It's all about choices and you can make them now - it's up to you which path you take and whether you believe anything I say but I would not tell you something I wasn't sure about.

I was overweight and unhealthy when I started my journey but as I learned how food affects us through my studies into eastern philosophy and medicine, my thinking changed almost immediately. What I learned was a shock and completely changed my previous thinking.

I lost weight and became healthy through conscious decisions to eat natural, healthy foods that would feed my mind and body. I want you to become conscious of everything you do in life because then you have freedom and choice.

The following chapters are to be used by those who wish to enhance their health and well-being. The information I am about to share with you has not been widely understood or used in western society. It is an ancient, lost secret art of rejuvenation and complete health. But it is not a substitute for medical help - if you have an illness you should seek proper medical advice. It is up to you how far you wish to proceed. Obtain as much information and help as possible before you practice this ancient art and above all please do not abuse the information and knowledge given to you.

20

Secret Teachings

In this chapter you will learn some untold secret teachings from not just eastern traditional healing systems but from ancient civilisations such as the Celts and Druids. Modern western society has taken man away from his natural ability to heal himself through rejuvenation and self-massage. Hermeticism has cloaked much of the essential teachings handed down to man from his earliest ancestors. The secret teachings are usually closed to modern man because if it were known, it could possibly be misunderstood and even worse misused.

I do not believe that ancient knowledge tombs like pyramids, cathedrals or pre-historic ruins such as Stonehenge have a built in timing device that will allow them to release hidden knowledge and wisdom. But I do believe that man will eventually know and understand the natural laws of the universe as he learns to once again listen to the voice of nature.

The modern student of esoteric philosophy concentrates mostly on Chinese philosophies with a big emphasis on oriental healing and medicine. What we are learning today is a far more advanced lost healing art called 'Do-In' or 'Mysterious Do-In'. It is the most mysterious of all human arts and none is more vital and important than its workings and energy. A truly unexplainable amount of strength and youthfulness that helps ward off illness and disease is the secret to this truly amazing art.

Where Was The Secret Held?

The art of Do-In has been used by most of the ancients in their golden age but most of the principal aspects of Do-In were buried and revealed to a chosen few and in some instances substituted by medical drugs and medical intervention.

Where did Do-In Surface Again?

It is told by late and present day sages that whatever knowledge is lost will in time return and become even stronger. This knowledge from previous generations can only resurface at the appropriate time and usually at one particular spot on earth; in time of course it will spread to other areas. Do-In resurfaced in the east and was only introduced to the west in a booklet a few years ago. The first book of Do-In and its translations sold over a million copies and caused an unusual amount of testimonials of self-healing.

How Does Do-In Work?

This gentle but energizing self-massage on certain parts of the body aids regeneration and healing. Using the same accu-points as acupuncture but applied slightly differently with fingertip strokes, the practice does not require you to have any special skills. Each step will be clearly shown and illustrated in nonmedical terms. This wonderful art can be done in the peace and quiet of your own home.

The techniques in this book are purely for self-application without tuition and without guidance from any professional. Do-In has been practiced successfully for thousands of years and was almost lost in time forever, Do-In has returned to help

mankind today.

However if you want to join our classes of Do-In to learn this ancient art from scratch, please get in touch. I hold classes throughout the north-west and private tuition is available on request.

Kid as in Kilt and Keltic, originated from this particular group of sages, however today the closed teachings of the Celts or Kelts have been rediscovered by investigation at the college of the Druids in Nanterre, France. The Druids did not write on their stones. Theirs was an Earth/Sky kind of science and it was learned by a student who stood by the proper time cycle of day in secret stone circles and received its cosmic wisdom in its purest of forms.

The stone circles and cromlechs developed out of a need to observe the forces of earth as they react to the influences of the sky, water and wind. The stones were very precise instruments in which the outer physical effects of those elements were shut off so that the Druids could study and feel the metaphysical flow force of his own body and mind. They would do this usually in a darkened room away from the bright rays of the sun or moon. In this relaxed, respective state, a bit like hypnosis, they would allow the Ki (Universal Energy) to penetrate their body and deepen their wisdom. Thus their bodies would be re-energized with all the natural forces of the universe.

Of course, this was a time when there were no books or clocks. To get information about sowing seeds, there was only the cosmos itself to read and learn from. This is when Druids would watch the action of the sun on its stones and read from nature more vividly than any book written today. In the shadow of these stones the sun spoke directly to them in complete Ideograms and nothing needed to be derived from his intellect.

Do-In would be practiced in the morning at sunrise, when they would observe the breathing in of the day, and the outer through their seven senses. Although the pulsating strength from the flow of Ki (Universal Energy) in their plexus was submitted to the dawning force, the inner stimulation was truly spiritual and would advance their wisdom.

Start Today

You can practice this anytime. There is no set time of the day or night that you need to do it because universal energy is there twenty four hours a day. Although some practitioners, especially in Japan and China, would practice this ancient art at day break. Start today and enjoy this lifelong mystical art of health and rejuvenation. It has been said that those who enjoy the Do-In way of life have far more energy and stamina than top performing athletes who eat and exercise in more conventional ways.

The Self Healing Exercise

The Secret Healing Tree

Have you ever noticed some city people who occasionally to nature yet seek solitude sitting under a tree with their bare feet? This inbuilt instinct is in us all but we have learned to close it off from everyday life.

Breathing is the strongest force of man and by sitting under the trunk of a tree you breathe in the wonderful secret curative healing effect. Two different stances are applied for best effect and if you choose to take the time out for this at least twice a week you will instantly notice differences in your health and well being.

1. Stand with the length of your backbone touching the bark of a tree. This heals the nervous system.
2. Standing with the chest and stomach in direct contact with the tree, your feet placed either side of the roots or a couple of feet away. This contact with the tree has a curative effect on the vegetative system: aiding your intake of air and digestion of food.

These are still practiced today in some very ancient martial arts known as "Kuatsu" or "Kappo". While I am not able to cover the full scope of the Do-In, this guide covers techniques which are highly regarded as invaluable after accidents. I mention these special Aikido teachings which are still alive and taught today in Hawaii, Japan, and the United States by some true masters whose techniques are derived from the principles of Do-In.

Another secret teaching which has fallen by the wayside are the techniques used to revive someone in shock, hit by a blow or similar. The techniques are by rapid, precise percussions, massaging and torsions, similar to those in the inductive massage techniques but applied with much greater force. In addition, special shouts in major keys producing harmonic sound waves induce excitation of cardiac and breathing functions, these are still taught today in the 21st century by high ranking black belt Judo players.

The scientific western mind can not conceive how internal organs can be influenced by the will; yet a traditional doctor trained in the ancient medical arts agrees that inner organs can be healed by Do-In.

As you practice the following self healing Do-In exercises you will begin to feel much more happy and alive than ever before, as if your body is singing with delight. The more you practice, the more in tune with your subconscious ability you will become and you will have far fewer illnesses and live longer.

Self Healing

All the self healing techniques described here can be done alone without any assistance. It is quite possible to do them as a family or with friends but either way you will grow physically and spiritually. However it is important to plan a time of day to follow the exercises, the morning at sunrise is best. However if that's not possible then choose another time of day that fits with your daily routine.

Before You Start

1. Choose time to exercise
2. Select a quiet place where you can't be disturbed, preferably outside facing east. If this is not possible find a room with the window open facing eastwards.
3. Always perform on an empty stomach
4. Calm the mind by taking a few deep breaths and exhaling fully.
5. Wear light clothing that is not tight or restricting.
6. Don't wear shoes unless you absolutely have to.
7. If you find the ground on the floor too hard then use a cushion or pillow.
8. Sit in the seiza position, this is sitting on the heels ; but if this is uncomfortable then sit how it is most comfortable for you

You are now ready

Exercise 1

Standing upright, bring the hands up to the ribcage, palms upward, elbows out. Inhale, breathe in through the nose with your mouth shut. Hold your breath, then slowly stretch one arm up and turn the palm upward, lift the head and look at the back of your hand. Lower the other hand downwards with the palms facing down and pull down hard on that side of the body. Slowly exhale. Relax and repeat on the other side of the body.

Exercise 2

Standing. Place your feet together, your big toes should be touching each other with the ankle bones tightly wedged against one another. Now exhale. Stretch both arms forward horizontally, fingers wrapping themselves around the rays of the sun and enclosing the" Ki" energy that emanates from it. Slowly inhale as you pull both hands up to the armpits. Lung acupoint: at the same time, alternatively lift the heels, rubbing the ankle bones together. This stimulates the acu-points 3-6 of the meridians.

Exercise 3
Salute the sun

Sit on your heels with your knees one fist apart. Inhale. Place your hands flat on the ground on either side of your thighs and slowly slide them forward while bending the trunk. Exhale and continue inclining the upper part of the body until the chest touches the knees; the hands are now forming a triangle, into which the forehead is placed, touching the ground. When your lungs are completely empty, remain in this position for a few moments longer before raising the trunk while inhaling and complete the movement, retuning slowly to the first position. Repeat this exercise at least three to six more times.

Exercise 4
The Scissors

Sit in the seiza position (see above). Exhale and compress the chest cavity by crossing both arms slowly. Uncross and raise the arms above the shoulders and towards the rear while inhaling. Allow the air to remain in the lungs. Exhale forcefully while quickly closing the arms and return to the first position.

Breathing Control

Correct breathing is a conscious and deliberate process and takes some special effort from you at the beginning. However this is only done gradually and you should not feel anxious when you don't get it right the first few times, it will come as you practice daily.

Exercise 5
Gathering Ki

Gather Ki energy through the fingertips in the seiza position. Hold your hands together just above eye level. Calmly inhale and rub the palms vigorously together until the fingers start to feel warm and the Ki begins to flow. Exert the greatest pressure you possibly can even if you get tired. To strengthen the heart, rub until you start to perspire in the armpits. Rub vigorously for about 1 minute.

Exercise 6
The Big Expeller

Again sitting in the seiza position. Link the fingers together of both hands, then cup them and rest them in your lap. Inhale and raise the buttocks from the heel. Bring the air that is trapped in the hands forcefully into the lower abdomen. Exhale, releasing the breath through the mouth at the same time. Lean the trunk of your body forward to maintain a soft belly.

Exercise 7
Hairline Stimulation

Start with all eight fingers digging into the hairline scalp. Move your forehead up and down with some force while taking in short deep breaths. Inhale, exhale, inhale, exhale... and so on.

Exercise 8
Pulling the Hair

This may seem rather strange. Grabbing your hair with both hands, pull your hair up and around the back with some force until the scalp starts to tingle. This aids kidney and bladder regeneration.

Exercise 9
Drumming Head

With your wrists flexible, allow the knuckles or the fingertips to drop rhythmically on the top and on the sides of the head. Very lightly drum the head (do not do this hard like pounding). Inhale throughout the exercise. This is good for the relief of constipation, haemorrhoids, prostate, kidney troubles and menstrual cramps.

Exercise 10
Neck Fanning

Stand tall in the seiza position. Inhale; bend the head forward very gently. With loose wrists and fingers arched backwards begin fanning upwards at a point between the shoulder blades or as low as you can possibly reach. This brings the Ki energy up from the lower spine to the upper neck and the brain nerve governor ruling the cerebral functions. This relieves nervous tension, improves speech, memory and facial mobility.

Exercise 11
Palms and Fingertips Neck

Place your right hand on top of the left hand and knead the muscles of the rear of the neck region until softened. Change the position of the hands with the left hand on top of the right and repeat. This stimulates the bladder and gall bladder meridians.

Exercise 12
Triple Warmer

Place both hands at the upper part of the back of the head and the thumbs digging into the nape, massage with the tips of the thumbs on the base of the skull. Accupoints that will be triggered are Tw 16, Gb 20, and Bv 10.

Exercise 13
The Neck

Kneading the side of the neck. Using the heel of the hands and the fingertips, squeeze and deeply massage the flesh of the neck area. This stimulates the following accupoints: Lig 16 to 18, Gb 21 and Tw 15.

Exercise 14
Head Rotating

Let the head slowly roll around, making full circles while holding the inhaled breath and then stop the rotation bend the head forward and exhale forcefully through the mouth. Repeat in the opposite direction. When difficulty in bending the head is experienced it indicates that the small intestine does not function properly.

Exercise 15

Inhale and hold the breath. Lower the head forward on to the chest until the chin touches it. Open the mouth and exhale forcefully. If pain is felt while doing the above head bend it indicates there is a lack of Ki (Energy) in the liver

Exercise 16
Looking Towards the Sky

Sit in the seiza position and inhale, holding the breath, drop the head and place your chin in the palm of one hand with the fingers pointing up along the mandible bone. The other hand is laid on top of the head very slightly to the back. Now firmly twist the head in the direction of the fingers of the lower hand and look up to the sky with the assistance of both your hands. Release the pressure quickly and exhale forcefully through the mouth. Return to the centre position and repeat two to three more times. Change the position of the hands and repeat three more times.

Exercise 17
The Head Twister

As you inhale, hold the breath and turn your head to the extreme right. Now exhale and return to the centre position. Repeat three times or more on either side.

Exercise 18
The Bow Twister

Sit in the seiza position with the spine very straight. Place both hands close together below the clavicle bone. Inhale and, as if you are stretching a bow, pull one arm out while holding the breath,Breathe in. Release "the arrow" and breath completely without tension. Rest and clasp the hands again to the chest and repeat, this exercise is said to regain the hearing, to restore the depleted kidneys, to simulate the blood flow in the spleen and stomach. It also relieves arthritis.

Exercise 19
Clearing the Lungs

Inhale as you allow the right hand to float upwards, your palm facing you as a mirror. Bring the left hand smartly up in the back of the right hand and wrap it around the right thumb. Hold the breath in and use the left hand to twist the right one with its palm facing outward (turn it counter clockwise) quickly bring both hands down to the navel, still twisted. Bend both hands forward, pointing the fingers towards the toes forcefully. Begin exhaling and stretch as far forward as possible, still keeping the twisting grip tight. Rest during one inhale/exhale cycle. Repeat three times on either side. The twisting of the arm and wringing of the hand forces the discharge of toxins and poisons.

Exercise 20
The Complete Belly Self Massage

You can stand for this exercise, drawing the feet upward, soles flat on the ground. With the intestines completely relaxed, place the palm of the hand flat on the stomach just above the navel, the other hand below. Move the hands in opposite directions with just enough pressure to lift the soft flesh up and down as well as sideways. Complete at least ten back and forth motions. Then place your hand on top of the other directly on over the navel. Inhale and hold the breath in the abdomen with some pressure, rotate the hands in a clockwise motion. After you have done this seven times, turn your head sideways and exhale noisily through the open mouth.

We have come to the end of the exercises for better health and it's now time for you to put it into practice. Of course these are only a few of the Do-In exercises and you can learn more about them through my website or joining one of my Do-In classes. But these few exercises will help you to experience much better healing.

21

The Happy Factor

We all know what it feels like to be happy. It's that feeling of being alive when something pleases us and that wonderful rush of serotonin in our bodies. Then there is the one when we feel at one with the universe, this is the state which we call 'the flow' or being 'in the zone'. Some great athletes feel this flow or even some musicians feel this way when they are playing music beautifully.

I feel in this zone when I'm writing or simply walking barefoot in the woods, I get a feeling of oneness with the universe. I get most of my inspiration at these times when I'm simply at one with nature. You will find that most of the greatest people that ever lived got their great ideas whilst in this state of being too.

We can all recognise this feeling because it's a bit like coming home. In western society we think we will be happy through external means. It goes a bit like this; 'I'll be happy when I'm a millionaire' or 'I'll be happy when I meet the man of my dreams'. Of course it's not your fault, because we are taught these things from an early age, but if you have read the papers lately or watched television you will clearly see this is not the case.

However in eastern tradition they are taught and believe that happiness is found from within, I believe this is a more accurate way of thinking, but I know that coming from the west it's difficult to understand that, when everything about your life seems clouded through lack of money and resources. I believe it good to have both, why not? Isn't life better when you have money? Well it's a damn site better than having none. You can have this state of mind more often when you start to let go of old habits that hold you back from achieving your true potential.

"If Happiness Is a State Of Mind Then I Want To Be In That State More Often"

You already know how to create these states from this book and you can start right now to experience this state of happiness more often.

Think what happiness feels like for you now. It could be a warm feeling of peace, tranquility or satisfaction. I don't know for sure what happiness feels like for you but I do know you can experience it more often. You can do this now by simply thinking of a time when you felt really happy or exhilarated about something or someone. As you go through the memory see what you saw, hear what you heard and feel all the good feelings associated with it. Now when that feeling is at its strongest press the thumb and finger of your right hand together and hold it there for a few moments.

Now let go of the thumb and finger as you relax. Next time you want to create that feeling of happiness simply press the thumb and finger together of the right hand again and experience that feeling all over again.

Smile into Your Life

Smiling has been said to save lives and I believe it; it's more powerful than you think. Imagine now what it would be like if every person you saw or bumped into on the street smiled at you. How wonderful that would be? Now whilst some of you may think it odd, really it isn't; just because you are not used to seeing people smiling all the time doesn't mean it's odd. In-fact it's odd not to.

Have you ever had a bad day and you're feeling lousy when suddenly someone just smiled at you for no apparent reason, didn't that make you feel instantly better. Think about it - when you smile you release the happy chemical serotonin in your body that makes you feel good, so next time you're feeling down, do yourself a favour and smile. Try it now, it works wonders.

If you are reading this book and you can hear and see and speak and walk you are definitely alive - so what have you got to be unhappy about? This means you have all the resources to make your life better.

Happiness is a state of mind and if you live your life every day in that state of happiness then you will feel good all of the time for no apparent reason. Now that's what I call taking control back.

Of course we can't predict what cards we are dealt all of

the time, so when something terrible happens in your life like a death of someone you love or a breakdown of a relationship it's only natural to feel down and cry, in fact this is necessary for you to heal properly. I can remember when my brother and then my dad both died within weeks of each other. I was only eleven when it happened and I felt the impact of losing two people who were so close and I loved dearly.

If you have just experienced either of these things and you are feeling low take heart in the fact that it's your body's way of healing. You must go through the process I call the 'vulnerability state' where even the mention of a particular place you used to go can cause you to be in floods of tears. Of course time is a great healer and eventually it subsides to a dull ache and eventually a distant memory. It is only natural you feel so overwhelmed at first because you are so used to being with that person but as time goes on and you start living without that person in your life, the pain of losing them lessens.

People often feel stupid or silly for crying and showing their vulnerability but actually it is a sign of strength. You will probably have noticed how people born in the Mediterranean all use their emotions much more than we Brits, I believe this is one of the reasons there is far less need for drug intervention and mental health problems in those countries. When you make use of all the senses you were born with and embrace them, your life will be more fulfilled.

You have a natural endorphin release when you do any physical exercise or laugh or even when you're resting, you know how good it can feel to come home from work on a cold winter's day and slip into a warm shower before you relax fully for the night. That feeling is your own body's endorphins working for you.

But endorphins are not just there to make you feel good; endorphins are neuro-transmitters that can create more connections in the brain and make you more intelligent, so when you experience your next endorphin release you also become more intelligent.

You can create more of these happy chemicals in your life in an instant by using the following techniques.

Your Own Endorphin Release

1. Remember a time in your life now when you felt completely happy, return to it now making the picture bigger, brighter and bolder, making sure as you do that you are in the picture not just an observer.
2. Now totally immerse yourself in those happy feelings and make them richer and fuller, bringing them up close.
3. Now notice where in your body these feelings are strongest and give the feelings a colour sending the colour up to the top of your head and down to the bottom of your feet - double and triple the brightness.
4. If you want you can imagine your endorphins as little fish swimming around in your blood stream and releasing a golden coloured liquid into your body.
5. Now repeat this again and again at least 4-5 more times.

You can create this fantastic feeling in your everyday life whenever you want to feel good. Of course, as with anything, take care to not be as high as a kite on endorphins in the middle of driving or anything else that takes concentration.

It's All about Oxygen

Ever wondered why the less active you are the more weight you put on even though you haven't changed your eating habits? Well it's simple really, the less active you become the less oxygen you have circulating around your body, the less fuel increases your blood flow. And that blood flow is what moves excess weight and fat. The reason Do-In exercises or other yoga type exercises is so effective is the primary focus on breathing. The bigger breaths maximize your lung capacity. As when you increase physical activity, the activity that bulks up the muscles, the cardiovascular activity that forces you to take big breaths is increasing your oxygen levels.

You can also add to that equation that any other exercise (like sex!) will also increase your serotonin (neurotransmitters) and endorphin production. These are the chemicals inside your body we already talked about that make you feel good and make you more intelligent. Higher levels of serotonin and endorphins also positively impact your ability to lose weight. Wow. So if you breathe more and feel great you will make it easier to lose weight.

So remember the next time you don't want to exercise or go out for a walk you are putting yourself at a higher risk to put more weight on.

Lower levels of serotonin are usually associated with mood disorders, particularly depression and certain drugs that are known as SSRIs (Selective Serotonin Reuptake Inhibitors) are used to treat BDD and other disorders mainly characterized by depression.

The human brain actually weighs about three pounds and

influences everything you do in your life. You may not realise it, but your brain is not the same today as it was yesterday, or even last week or last month. The brain is continually changing and making new cells, when you learn something new, or have experienced new things in your life, new synapses form in the brain. Some synapses get stronger, while others disappear. Your brain allows you to feel pleasure whenever you do something you like, such as reading a book, meeting friends or making love. The reward pathway has been activated and the stimulation of the neurons that make serotonin get a serotonin release making you feel good.

22

The Trouble with Psychology

Psychology never really helped me that much. Why? Because in my opinion, it's got it all wrong. You can't help someone by going back into the past and blaming someone, or something for their current behaviour, you can only help someone by eliminating the unpleasant memories of the past. As the saying goes 'you can't fix a problem in the same state of mind it was created' so doesn't it make sense to change your state of mind and in doing so you change the outcome?

I have another problem with psychology. Now I don't know about you but I have never been able to respond to someone who is detached and has no idea of what they are doing with you other than what they have been taught from a text book. How do I know this? Because I've experienced it many times. I can remember many years ago when I had a breakdown and was sent to see a psychologist the first thing he said to me was if you don't take the pills we give you and you are still unstable then you can't get any more help.

'Wow!' I thought, how the hell was this supposed to be

helping me. In fact what it did do was once again confirm in my mind that there was something wrong with me and I should just shut up once again because 'they' know best right? Wrong! Very wrong!! Even worse he was effectively saying I shouldn't expect anything better from life.

Of course now I understand that what they were really saying was 'look if you don't play it our way and stop showing your emotions then we don't want to know'. Ironically, no one came to talk to me in all the time I was in hospital; all I was given was anti-depressants to suppress the symptoms and if I took them like a good little girl they would then take all the credit for my return to health and if I didn't, it was my fault not theirs.

Well I think we all know that anti-depressants do not fix the problem - all they do is mask it and alter one's state of mind; I can remember feeling like a vegetable for the few short months I was taking them and I have to say I felt like a lid had been lifted when I stopped taking them and I vowed never ever to get myself into that situation again.

Any kind of drugs act on the neurons in your brain. Drugs release a chemical called dopamine, this increased rush of dopamine gives the user a rush or high that can be enjoyable for a short time. But drugs can cause other changes to the brain that could last a very long time.

With drug abuse a person usually develop cravings. If a person takes drugs and then stops taking them, he or she will crave them. In other words he or she will have an overwhelming desire to take them. Drugs have such a strong effect on the human brain that even the mention of them can trigger an abuser to want them.

I knew then that the world was full of people in high ranking professions who had no idea what they were doing to other people and worst of all, they didn't seem to care. Why do I say this? Because if they did had then they would be willing to learn from their mistakes and change the things that don't work. We are born to learn every day of our lives, no one is perfect and no one will ever know everything but it's this hierarchical attitude that prevents people from learning.

Psychology is so far out of touch it's untrue and it needs to take a long good look at what it is projecting onto people – it's a dangerous combination of arrogance and ignorance in my opinion. Wouldn't it be great if we could all accept that we can learn something new every day of our lives? It's given me years of pleasure knowing I can learn something more about people and their behaviour every day of my life and in doing so I get to help people – or rather it's not me that helps them, I just show them another way to help themselves - it's all down to them.

I know there will be people in the medical profession who don't believe in my methods but I don't care because I know my own methods work. You can't argue with facts and I have proof of my work helping people and I have proof of how mainstream psychology doesn't. This is in no way a personal attack on individual psychologists it's more an opinion on psychotherapy and how it's taught. After all, who says that the way they teach you is right? Do we ever question who says so, whether there is proof? People are generally very trusting and that's a good thing but you have to start asking more questions it's your life... Psychology teaches people to bury their emotions and mask them with drug intervention so how on earth can it be right?

My methods teach people how to recognise when they have a problem and to eliminate it from their life. My methods teach people to not be concerned with why we do it but how to stop doing it. If I have stirred some emotion inside you whilst reading this statement and that emotion has made you question other people's beliefs, including mine, then I have done my job.

It would be sad to think that what I told you wasn't backed up with some solid proof. I have a way of knowing this because I make sure I stay in touch with all my clients and ask them to tell me how they feel, but most importantly I can see the changes in them as they happen.

"If you look closely you will see"

I am afraid for our future generation of geniuses. They seem to be a dying breed through poor choices and lifestyles. The geniuses who we so fondly remember such as Einstein, Plato, Franklin, Edison, Lincoln, Mozart and many others will become but distant memories or forgotten forever if we continue on our present course. More importantly will we have a future generation of these true geniuses? I fear not if we continue with the choices we make and the poor lifestyle we choose to live.

Any future generation of geniuses will have to have health and well being on their side otherwise they will be non-existent. Should our present generation remain ignorant of foods to feed the mind and body and only eat processed foods in their diet, how can they attain such a grand status? When you eat badly it keeps you poor in every sense of the word. Poor thinking, poor health and an unfruitful life.

I know many people will think this a bold statement and it is but I believe it to be true. If the food you eat feeds your mind and body then it has to be of a certain quality, you wouldn't give the wrong kind of fuel to your car would you? Because if you did it would soon break down, yet people give the wrong kind of fuel to their bodies on a daily basis and encounter all kinds of problems with their health until one day the body has had enough shit running through it and gives up.

Health is an education and it requires you to grasp the basics. You can advance your studies and become super healthy. I know it's hard not to believe what the so called professionals or food chains are telling you because they have the money and resources to market their products very well, and spend billions of pounds every year to promote their products so that you will go out and buy them.

You have to be resilient and stand out from the crowd and say no to processed foods that are killing you slowly. Do you think they eat it? I leave it to your own imagination.

I wish you love peace and happiness in your quest to find health.

23

The Magic Gland

The pineal gland is a tiny pine cone shaped gland that can be found at the back of the third ventricle of the brain. Ventricles are fluid filled spaces within the brain. The functions of the pineal gland are not fully understood by some scientists. But one function that is understood is this gland's production of the hormone melatonin. Melatonin is involved in the regulating of the body's 'internal clock' controlling when you sleep and when you wake up.

The role of this gland has long been contemplated by philosophers. Ancient Greeks believed the pineal gland was our connection to the realms of thought. Descartes called it the seat of the soul. The gland also controls the biorhythms of the body in response to day and night (light and dark). It works in harmony with hypothalamus which is responsible for the body's thirst, hunger, sexual desire and the biological clock that determines the ageing process.

Changes With Age

The pineal gland is large in children but shrinks at puberty. It appears to play a role in sexual development and hibernation in animals - the high melatonin level in children is believed to inhibit sexual development until puberty arrives and melatonin production is reduced. This could account for behavioural problems in adolescents. The pineal gland is responsible for both normal and abnormal puberty.

Descartes' remarks about the pineal gland generated a lot of interest in 1640. He wrote a lot of letters to answer a number of questions raised. He explained why he thought it was the principal seat of the soul, saying:

"In my view this is indeed the principal part of the soul, and the place in which all our thoughts are formed. The reason I believe this is that I cannot find any part of the brain, except this, which is not double. Since we only see with one thing with two eyes, and hear only one voice with two ears, and in short only ever have one thought at a time, it must necessarily be the case that the impressions which enter by the two eyes or by the two ears, and so on, unite with each other in some part of the body before being considered by the soul. Now it is impossible to find any such place in the whole head except this gland; moreover it is situated in the most suitable place for this purpose, in the middle of the concavities and it is supported and surrounded but little branches of the carotid arteries which bring the spirits into the brain".

(29TH JANUARY 1640, AT III:19-20 CSMK 143).

174

And as he wrote later that same year,

> *"Since it is the only solid part in the whole brain which is*
> *single, it must necessarily be the seat of the soul, for one cannot*
> *be separated from the other. The only other alternative is to say*
> *that the soul is not joined then to any solid part of the body,*
> *but only to the animal spirits which are in the concavities, and*
> *which enter it and leave it continually like the water of a river.*
> *That would certainly be thought of as too absurd."*

(DECEMBER 1640)

Only a few people accepted Descartes pineal neurophysiology when he was still alive and it was almost universally rejected when he died.

Scientific Development

Scientific studies of the pineal gland made little progress until the nineteenth century. As late as 1828 a lot was said about the pineal gland and then the situation started to change when several scientists independently launched hypotheses claiming that the pineal gland is a phylogenic relic, a vestige of a dorsal or third eye. A modified theory of this is still accepted today. Scientists also began to surmise that the pineal gland is an endocrine organ. This hypothesis was fully established in the twentieth century. The hormone secreted by the pineal gland, melatonin, was first isolated in 1958. Melatonin is secreted in a circadian rhythm, which is interesting in view of the hypothesis that the pineal gland is a vestigial third eye. Melatonin was hailed as a wonder drug in the 1990s and then became one of the best sold health supplements. The history of the pineal gland research in the twentieth century has indeed received some attention from philosophers of science - (Young 1973, McMullen 1979).

Pseudo-Science

As philosophy reduced the pineal gland to just another part of the brain and science studied it as one endocrine gland among many, the pineal gland continued to have an exalted status in the realm of pseudo-science. Towards the end of the nineteenth century, Madame Blavatsky, the founder of theosophy, identified the third eye discovered by comparative anatomists of her time with the eye of Shiva of the Hindu mystics and concluded that the pineal gland of modern man is an atrophied vestige of this 'organ of spiritual vision'. (Blavatsky 1818, vol.2, pp.289–306). This theory is still alive today.

The pineal gland, as already mentioned, is a pine cone shape gland and it is therefore interesting to find this symbol of a pine cone as the biggest statue in the Vatican square? Also the pope's staff is embossed with the same shape of the pine cone. Why then does this shape appear in every ancient religion in the world? In Egypt, the symbols on the sphinx are known as the Eye of Horus. Look closely on the American dollar bill and there is also a third eye.

The Dollar Bill

In the physical body your eyes look outward - although they view objects upside down. It sends the message of what it observes to the brain which interprets the image and makes it appear right side up to us. But the human body has another physical eye, whose function has long been recognised by humanity. It is called the 'Third Eye' – the Pineal Gland. It is the Spiritual Third Eye, our Inner Vision, and it is considered the Seat of the Soul. It is located in the geometric centre of the cranium.

The Windows of the Soul:

To understand that the eye is the window to the soul, there are 2 techniques you can use, alone or with others.

Alone: Stand in front of a mirror in the dark. Shine a torch below your face pointing upward. Now stare at the eyes in the mirror and you shall see your image change into many people, some may not be human, all of whom are aspects of your soul experiencing in other grids.

Two People: Sit across from the person in a dimly lit or dark room. Place the torch below your face again. This will enable the other person to see you in other lives and tell you what they see as they look through the windows of your soul. They may also see themselves in that lifetime with you. Next repeat this by looking into the other person's eyes.

It is important not to move while doing this exercise. To be truly skilled at this, you will take the other person, or yourself, to their soul or 'spark of light'. It is the flicker of light: white, blue and purple, that you sometimes see in the periphery of your field of vision. Always remember, your experience here is just that... a second.

The pineal gland has been supplied with the very best blood supply, oxygen and nutrient mix. It acts as a receiving port capable of monitoring electro-magnetic fields, with its central hormone, Melatonin the pineal not only regulates our sleep cycles and the ageing process but also mysteriously acts as the mistress gland (Sophia) orchestrating the body's entire endocrine system and through energy the chakra system. I also believe it is responsible for shamanic states and visions.

The pineal gland is also unique in so much as it sits alone in the brain where others parts are paired. It is miraculously the first thing to be formed in the foetus and is distinguishable at just three week's gestation. When our individual life force enters our foetal body at just seven weeks, the time when we become truly human, it passes through the pineal and triggers the first flood of DMT (N-Dimethyltryptamine). Later on at birth, the pineal releases more DMT. DMT is also capable of mediating pivotal experiences of deep meditation, shamanic states of consciousness, psychoses, spiritual emergence and near death experiences.

The pineal gland starts to harden with calcified tissue starting around adolescence. These rather strange calcified deposits between 3-5mm are called 'brain sand'. There are asymmetrical crystals in the pineal gland that are piezo- electric that is, they send out electronic voltage creating EM waves. Whenever a person is exposed to EMF (electro-magnetic field) such as that of the earth the gland vibrates, sending out EM signals to the rest of the body. When the gland is stimulated geo-magnetically it produces alkaloids similar to plant psychedelics. Any change in the earth's EMF will produce a rush of psychedelics in our bodies enabling us to be more psychically active in our shamanic states (earth/land/respective) the pineal gland is affected by coherent EM fields and it can change its hormone production when exposed to EM at low levels. As the earth has the greatest effect on our physiology it makes perfect sense that the cells of our brain align with it. All life within the earth's vibration influence attempts to match base frequencies (entrainment) with that of the earth. To this day each one of our cells is consistently shifting and moving energy to achieve harmonic resonance with the reference signals of earth. Our bodies are truly amazing and they are intimately co-dependant with earth. Our bodies are miraculous organs of phenomenal complexity and outstanding ability.

We are made up from trillions of molecules and each one vibrates with its own intelligence, all inter-linked, just as the universe is inter-linked. We can reflect the whole. A picture may begin to emerge with you now about your own infinite wisdom and how you can experience your own shamanic state through the wisdom of your body in tune with the earth.

When we experience a shamanic state our pulse rate increases at the same time as our blood pressure drops. This is also what happens as the body is preparing to die. As the life force leaves our body through the pineal gland, another flood of DMT is released. I believe that the shamanic state replicates that of a near death experience and so triggers the DMT release in the brain.

I believe that shamanic work when combined with breath work brings large amounts of oxygen and life force into the blood stream and, because of its extraordinary blood supply, the pineal gland receives large proportions of stimulation from the oxygen or prana in the blood system causing it to resonate/ vibrate thereby stimulating the DMT.

Ancient people knew the importance of the pineal gland. Magician, Delores Ashcroft-Nowak says that to the priests of

Heliopolis, the embalmers of ancient Egypt (who were the forerunners of today's pathologists), the Star Chamber of Isis (the Holy of Holies) and the Halls of Anubis and Thoth were not just fanciful terms given to mythical locations but were actually places within the living brain where the priests and priestesses travelled to be taught by the gods.

Tantric techniques attempt to produce enlightenment through sexual ecstasy. Pineal DMT release can mediate sexual ecstasy resulting from the over exertion, intense emotions and pneumocatharthis (intense dynamic breathing). It is known that psychedelic features can and do emerge during orgasm. The link between conscious waking state and deep Shamanic consciousness is bliss/rapture, feelings associated with intense sexual pleasure.

> **NOTE:** The secret sex techniques of the Shamanka (female shaman) still in practice in certain rural areas of Brazil, Mexico and South America all, generally, involve breathing techniques.

Our present scientific view is seriously challenged when we embark on shamanic journeys. When our consciousness expands beyond the boundaries of time and space we experience a wonderful limitless universe; a dazzling journey through inner space. We learn that our brain chemistry allows us access to other realms of existence - identification with our ancestors, animals, plants, encounters with intelligent non-human presences, fairies, spirits, elementals, angels, mythical beasts… The possibilities are endless and always fantastic. The experiences are profound and enlightening.

24

Mind and Body Awareness

Your mind and body are continually being influenced by conscious and subconscious reactions. In your lifetime, the mind will be continuously affected by the body and the body will be continually affected by the mind - both on a conscious and subconscious level. Think of your mind as a muscle to be developed just as you would by going to the gym and working out your leg or arm for a few hours.

When you've been working out for a few weeks there will be noticeable improvements to your overall health and well being then, after a few months, you will have reached an acceptable level of fitness to either carry on and become super fit or give up and pat yourself on the back for having done so well and take a break.

Most people will give up and congratulate themselves for having come this far but the ones who want more from life and themselves will carry on, not only to become good or super fit but until they become the best at what they do or better still the best in the world.

If any of the above habits above apply to you then ask yourself this question – how good do you really want to be? Average, good, quite good, the best, the best in your field, or the best in the world? So you can see all improvement takes time and energy and most important of all a steely determination to reach the top.

You are the perfect example of a wonderful human being – why not use the God given talents you were born with? Why settle for second best when you can be the best?

Develop your mind power so that when you achieve great things in your own life you will be a perfect example to others who want to achieve the same. Don't hide your abilities and talents for what use is that? Show them to the world and continually update your mind to bigger and better things.

Mental Relaxation Exercise

To get clarity on any situation or to advance your mind power you will need to learn how to control your mind and focus fully on your goals. Find yourself a few hours (just an hour will do) to fully relax. Start by sitting comfortably in a quiet room where you will not be disturbed.

> Breathe deeply in and out at least three to five times and as you begin to relax, notice your muscles relaxing further and count from 100 all the way down to zero telling yourself all the time you feel really comfortable and relaxed now.
>
> It doesn't matter if you get lost as you count - you will drift in and out of a hypnotic state for a while - thoughts just pop in and out of your mind. Don't try to stop them just allow your mind to go where-ever it chooses.

Now visualise yourself doing what it is you have found impossible to do in the past, see it clearly as if it were happening right now... then step into the visualisation and feel all the good feelings associated with it.

Because the subconscious mind doesn't know the difference between a real or imagined experience, your mind will think it is real and if you keep on repeating this simple exercise you are re-setting the thermostat for more success in your life. As the days and weeks go by you will begin to notice profound changes as you have created more of your own luck in life. Don't be too surprised if you actually get what you want.

Remember everything you want to attract into your life should first begin in the imagination before it can manifest into reality.

"Excellence is an art won by training and habit. We do not act rightly because we have virtue or excellence, but rather we have those because we have acted correctly. We are what we repeatedly do. Excellence, then, is not an act but a habit."

ARISTOTLE

Getting Over the Poverty Mindset

It's not your fault if you're one of the poverty conscious people who believe being rich is something other people do and not you. Unfortunately schools don't teach people how to be rich, they teach you how to work for someone else, and if you work hard enough you could end up with a top paying job.

I should know because I was one of them!

Of course the more I educated myself, the more confidence I had and the more I began to realise that I could actually do or be anything I wanted to be. So having millions if not billions of pounds was not something other people did anymore it was something I could have too.

Once I decided what it was I wanted to do and then become the best I could possibly be I would then be in a position to earn vast amounts of money for myself as much as I wanted, there is no limit to this because, contrary to popular belief, it's not that there isn't enough money to go round anymore in fact the pot just gets bigger and bigger.

Yes, it's hard to digest at first that this kind of wealth is really available to you and everyone who cares to have it, because you've been living all these years thinking unconsciously that you simply don't have what it takes to become super rich. You would be wrong!!

It's time to take stock of your life and really think about what it is you want to do. Because when you're doing something you love, rather than doing something because you have to, it makes all the difference to the outcome for both you and your loved ones.

Think about it, would the person who loves you most want you to be unhappy? The answer is probably not. I know some of you are thinking 'Well it's ok for you to talk but I've got a mortgage to pay and two kids to feed', and you're right – I've been there. But for years I was so unhappy working for someone else earning what can only be described as a pittance, after the tax man had taken his slice and the shopping bills had been paid, not to mention the clothes bill all year round for three kids left pretty much nothing left to enjoy life with. So I decided it's going to be no more hard to train and get to be where I want to be, than living on the bread line for the rest of my life – for me it was a big deal not to.

I could not have lived with myself if I continued to live my life like that just to please other people and keep the rent paid. it wasn't like it was forever I could still pay the rent and food in my cupboards and as long as I knew the end result would be profoundly better for me and my family I could put up with it for a while longer, after all I had been doing it for years anyway with nothing to show at the end of it.

I can't tell you how much my life changed after I had realised how much of my behaviour was unconscious. I can remember when I first advertised my services as a therapist I made more money in that first month than I had made in three months at my previous job and I was my own boss. From there on my life began to change for the better and fortunately my family supported me all the way. They had seen my determination and as they all got older my confidence and determination affected them in the best possible way. They too became smart, intelligent human beings who had the confidence to go out and do what they wanted in life.

Now they are all grown up and have their own lives, I have had the great fortune to stay close to my children, I believe directly through my own changes. Isn't it great to think you can have a huge positive impact on your children's lives as they grow into adults?

I began to teach these techniques I had learned to my clients and friends and very soon they too began to change for the better.

Some research has shown that a large proportion of people who suddenly come in to money from a lottery win or an inheritance will actually lose it and go back to having nothing. That same research suggests that they will in fact end up worse off than they originally were. And the reason is they still feel poor inside.

It's like a self-fulfilling prophecy: what we expect to be true in our minds will become true in the cold light of day. We act out our day to day life consistently as we did prior to the windfall, which means nothing has changed unconsciously, and your mind will find ways to spend it or get rid of it as quickly as you got it, because you feel unworthy of such large sums of money.

If you believe in your heart that you can't become wealthy, then you won't have to change your thinking unconsciously to manifest it in consciousness. We have been taught from birth that money is the root of all evil and that if you do have it, you should feel guilty for having it.

This kind of nonsense will keep you poor. You've probably heard the common terms for rich people many times like 'filthy rich' or 'fat cat' and another common belief is all rich people are liars - who made that one up I wonder?

What is even more absurd is the Catholic Church made poverty out to be something one should aspire to be and glad your soul was saved from damnation for wanting more, yet the Vatican is one of the richest businesses on the planet. We need to look at religion as a business and a very lucrative one at that.

I came from a big Catholic family and my father was very strict - he believed wholly in these old beliefs, not because he directly chose to believe in them but because he had them implanted in his unconscious mind by his parents. I often wonder what my father would think of my radical views on life now if he were alive? I believe he would have one day realised it was all clever trickery from people in high places like religious organizations. He was essentially a clever man and I'm sure we would have had some exciting conversations together.

It's time to start letting those old unwanted, outdated beliefs about yourself and that of your finances go and create new healthy foundations for the future. As you start on your new journey in life you will soon rid yourself of all the old programmes you've been running on for years and reprogram yourself to have more success and prosperity.

Have you ever noticed how some people seem to turn everything they touch into gold, while others seem to be stuck in a never ending spiral of poverty? So here is something I learned whilst I was in the process of change that - what you resist persists.

Some people really do deprive themselves from getting rich by their deep-rooted beliefs about money. No matter how hard they consciously try getting rich, their unconscious beliefs will not support them. Whoever said the conscious mind was the boss got that one wrong didn't they? So time to change your unconscious thinking before it becomes conscious reality.

How do I do that?

Well just the same way I described to you before in the previous chapter on how to mentally relax. First find a nice quite room where you can't be disturbed – make it clear in your mind what it is you want to do and how you're going to do it. ie. Where, when, and how - it's a bit like having a road map. You wouldn't set out on a journey without one would you?. Plan what you want to do, how you will go about getting it, check that no one will get hurt on the way, such as loved ones. Then take action to start it in motion.

Your plan should be like a business plan or a road map because you need to know how you will get there. You can add or take things away as and when required just as long as the basic plan is set in stone.

Don't forget to stop and take stock of your actions from time to time and check everything is going according to plan, if there are things that need to be changed or adjusted then please feel free to do it as soon as possible and get things back on track.

It's helpful to check your route to success about every three to six months to see how far you have come from the beginning of your journey. If you have done something every day towards your goal then you can relax and be sure you are on target and it's only a matter of time before you reach your destination.

Sometimes people reach their destination much quicker than anticipated. This varies from person to person because no-one knows how much they want something to happen more than you and if you follow all the rules and go the extra mile needed for quicker success then you will without fail reach it much quicker.

Follow these golden rules for success

- Decide what you want
- Make a map or route of how to get there.
- Visualise it in your mind daily.
- Take action towards your goal.
- Do one thing every day towards your goal.
- Keep your eye on the end result.

I remember something a very dear friend once said when he was told the computer he was working on wasn't working properly. He said 'well you only get out what you put in, so if you put rubbish in you only get rubbish out'. It still brings a smile to my face when I think of that because it's true – your brain works in exactly the same way, if you put rubbish in then only rubbish can come out!

Your brain really is the most advanced computer in the world and the average person will only ever use less than half it's true capacity – so think how much more there is to learn about yourself. You better get a move on if you want to get to the next level, let alone use its full capacity.

I know some people who are driven to be rich through fear of poverty. Literally they are so driven because the thought about going back to having nothing would just be too upsetting. In my opinion, it is better to strive towards success not run away from something. Forget the fear, get rid of it through what you've learned in this book on how to set the subconscious mind up for success and slowly you can rid it of all the past beliefs that consistently held you back.

By focusing on poverty or lack of money you will attract more of it but if you start to focus on wealth and money and all that is available to you, then you will attract more of that, it's the universal law – what you focus on, you get more of.

Some people stay poor because it's more comfortable to stay in what they have known but wait a minute think of this? If you get to the end of your life on this planet, having done nothing more than what you currently think and believe – how will you feel? It costs nothing to try something new and usually there are huge benefits to changing what you've always done. We are not on this planet to stay small, for that is useless, we were all born to shine. Of course it's up to you how bright you want to shine, it's a bit like being a soap star or a big Hollywood movie star. If you want to shine you might as well turn up the brightness and be one of the brightest stars in the sky.

"Belief creates the actual fact"
WILLIAM JAMES

Years ago I can clearly remember reading Paul McKenna's self help book and in it he would tell how he would constantly worry about his lack of money, until he realised what he was doing and changed his thinking to that of wealth. He goes on to describe how he would imagine himself wealthy and then how he made a wealth scrap book by putting inside it all the people he wanted to meet, all the places he wanted to go, and all the money he visualised already having.

When I read it I thought I might give it a try, so made my own wealth scrap book and I have to say that it works wonderfully. It's a constant reminder of how far you've come on your journey. Why not try it for yourself? You might just be surprised how such a small thing can make a big difference.

25

The Study of Wealth

If you want to become wealthy then you should try spending some time with people who have already become wealthy. I found that asking wealthy people advice on how they did it certainly worked for me. Most people will help you if they think you are serious and actually offer their advice. Research who you believe could help you the most, you might even already know someone who has acquired great wealth and never thought to ask them for help. Now is a good time. If you don't know anyone directly, seek them out. Everyone has access to the internet, all it takes is a bit of research and you will find them, look for clips in newspapers or magazines about their wealth and then use it to your advantage, cut out the clippings. If there's a contact number call them and ask them about how they became so wealthy. I've always found that whenever I've asked for help people will be only too willing to offer advice and guidance, it comes natural to help our fellow human beings. But if they don't offer help or advice don't give up just keep going eventually you will find someone willing to talk to you.

I personally found clippings of all the wealthiest people on the planet and people I liked including, Bill Gates, Sir Richard Branson, Donald Trump, Oprah Winfrey and Paul McKenna just because I liked him and knew he had made himself a multi millionaire quite quickly.

I would cut newspaper clippings about them and read books about them or watch programmes whenever they appeared on TV. All this helped me to form a picture in my own mind of how they thought and acted.

I would then put them all in my wealth scrapbook and just kept adding to it every time there was news about their wealth. I also used the internet to search for information and print out any news that would be worthy of my wealth scrap book. I also used a friend's wealth advice and add that to my ever growing scrap book too. Eventually I found I could afford to live in an area that was wealthy so I had more chance of bumping into a few millionaires on my path to success. My own finances just kept growing by the day on my quest to reach my own true potential.

Creating financial wealth isn't easy because as any serial entrepreneur will tell you, there are risks to making money, but as the saying goes, anything worth having has a risk attached to it and some of us are braver than others. My suggestion is to build up a little nest egg before you take the risks, this will make the risk seem far less when you actually do take the bull by the horns and take the risks needed to create financial wealth.

I can remember a friend who had wanted to expand his business and looked at buying a small internet business that had been up for grabs in the area he wanted. He eventually met up with the owner of the business who told him if he wanted it then that was the price but that there was someone else interested in the business too and needed an offer on the table within a fortnight. My friend sadly lost out to the other interested party because he wasn't able to find the courage to take the risk due to limited resources. If he had bought the business it would have left him struggling financially for a while at least, but the other buyer didn't have the same dilemma – he was financially secure and to him it was a risk worth taking.

I later found out the buyer had made a very clever move in buying that little business because it earned him over £2.4 million profits in two years. If he had not been so worried about his current financial situation, my friend could have easily been £2.4 million better off today. You see lack of money can also lead us to making the wrong decisions, that's why I've always said it's easier to think of moving towards money rather than the lack of it before making a decision that could alter your life forever.

Warren Buffet is said to be worth $62bn and is the richest man in the world. The richest women in the world is Christie Ruth Walton aged 54 said to be worth $20bn. She is the wife of the late John T Walton who amassed his fortune from the well known supermarket chain Wall-mart better known to us here as Asda. She inherited his fortune after his death in June 2005.

What is interesting is that on research these billionaires all share the same school of thought regarding wealth. Warren Buffet said you may be tempted to spend the money you earn when you first start out but don't. Invest it back into yourself or your product or service or both. Buffet learned this very early on in his career at school. He and a friend bought a pinball machine to put in a barber shop and with the money they earned they bought more machines until they had eight of them in different barber shops. When they sold the business Buffet invested his share into another business and by the age of 26 he had amassed a fortune of $1.4 million in today's money, so you can see how even a small amount can turn into vast amounts of wealth if you know what you're doing.

Don't be afraid to be different. It's better to stand out in a crowd, not in one. When Warren Buffet started investing money many people thought he was an odd ball and that he would fail. He worked in Omaha not Wall Street and when he closed his partnership 14 years later it was worth more than $100 million. Instead of him following the usual crowd he looked for undervalued investments and ended up beating the market value each year. To Warren Buffet and many other wealthy people average is just that and being rich is no average thing. You need to measure yourself by judging yourself by your own standards not the world's.

Decisions/Indecisions

Just as important when you're making business or even personal decisions – don't hang about, make up your mind and move on. Warren Buffett prides himself on this quality by gathering all the information needed, even asking family members or friends to get you to stick to a deadline, then swiftly making up his mind and moving on. Unnecessary pondering is not useful and will hinder your decisions in the end.

Never Give Up

If you're going to become rich you need to know one thing and that is not giving up on the dream. Stay in control and be persistent even if some other company or service is bigger than yours, being persistent pays off in the end. Having tenacity and ingenuity will even sometimes win over the more established businesses or services.

What does success really mean to you?

Despite Warren Buffet's success he does not measure success by the dollar. In 2006 he had pledged to give away almost his entire fortune to charities, saying "when you get to my age you measure your success in life by how many of the people you want to have love you actually do love you". Surely, that's the ultimate test on how you've lived your life.

I think he is a wise man. He has also said, "Life is a playground and if you know and understand the rules you get to have great wealth and friendships for the time you're on this planet." Which translates, if we live our lives honestly, and preserve rather than destroy the planet we live on, everything will come to us that which we seek.

Risk It All

For me everything in life has a risk attached to it. It's a risk when you meet someone and get married, equally our emotions tell us 'this is the one' because we believe ourselves to be in love, and that nothing could possibly go wrong. Sadly, we know that is not true because of all the millions of divorced people walking the planet. Then some people try it again or even a third or fourth time at finding the right person, while others sadly only try it once and allow that one bad experience to spoil their whole lives and never marry again.

Optimism is everything, natural optimists will always fall on their feet because they don't give up on life, they are always looking for the next opportunity to take them to their dream, and in my estimation no matter how long it takes they will nearly always get there in the end. You have a choice. You can choose to see the cup half empty or to see it half full.

The 80/20 Rule

You have probably heard of Wilfred Pareto, who was one of the first people to point out that approximately 80 per cent of the world's wealth was owned by 20 per cent of the world's population. This rule is often found in all areas of life especially where major decisions are to be made. Just as 80 per cent of results come from 20 per cent of your efforts. If we focus all our attention on that 20 per cent throughout our own lives we get to have more of what we want.

Remember passion and excitement are all you need to take with you on the road to success, because when you have passion for what you do and there is excitement in it, people will be drawn to you, they will see your passion and optimism. They see what they too so desire and look to your passion to confirm they too can do it.

26

Stay Healthy

Staying healthy is a must if you want to become wealthy – it's part of the deal and you have to uphold it. If you look after your health you will feel good and be in the best position to make good decisions when you need to. Invest in your health and treat it as a priority in your life.

If you become unwell, you are far likelier to make bad decisions and become unstable in your dealings with people unable to perform to their optimum. It's easy to become careless when you feel under the weather or ill, I'm not saying we don't all get a cold from time to time but if it's more than that and more often then you need to look at your current lifestyle, your diet, your drinking habits and so forth. If you think it could be a problem, seek help appropriately. Remember happiness is a state of mind and body.

Living the Secrets to a Happier Life

When I think of happiness I think of all the exciting, wonderful things I have yet to learn and discover – do you know what it's like to be abundantly happy? In western society we often measure happiness by material things such as the acquisition of financial wealth. After all, we are taught from an early age that these things are to be admired and that they will ultimately make us happy.

Unfortunately this is only part of the story. Eastern tradition teaches that happiness comes from within and I have to say for me I think that is spot on. I think that these traditional eastern values were part of our own culture many years ago.

I know of a lot of people who are still waiting for external things to happen that they think can make them happy. I remember feeling totally devastated when my 16 year old brother and my dad died. Yet while I felt terrible I couldn't help thinking about the positive side. After all my brother and my dad would not want me to spend my life filled with sadness and being unhappy. Yes, I had to go through the crying stage because it is our natural emotion to cry for someone we have loved so much and I willingly went through this stage without rushing it but I also knew when it was time to stop and be thankful for having them in my life and find the most wonderful memories to keep with me instead of lamenting the fact that they were no longer here.

My message is - even in the worst circumstances we can find a smile. Some happiness or small memory to remind us we can live again. I knew even in my darkest hour that they would not want me to spend my whole life being sad. It's ok to be happy and smile even when circumstances tell you it's not appropriate. Be kinder to yourself, nothing bad is going to happen to you because you can find a smile. amongst the confusion and fear of it all. When you smile the world will smile back at you.

A smile can act like an aspirin, it can relieve your bad feelings so I encourage you to smile more often. Why not make it a New Year's Resolution or just a promise to yourself that for the next 10 days you will smile at everyone you see and watch what happens... Smiling will not only make everyone you meet feel wonderful but it will resonate throughout your whole body and make you feel alive.

I was once taught by my Japanese teacher that when we smile into our own hearts and minds we have learned the secrets to long lasting health and happiness. Smiling at your heart and every organ in the body at the same time is sending love to it bringing a sense of well-being to your soul.

Why not try it for yourself?

- Relax in a chair or lie down where you won't be disturbed.
- Take some deep breaths.
- Close your eyes when your relaxed.
- Now imagine kissing your heart and sending it love.
- Do the same with your brain send it love and kisses.
- And the same to your liver & kidneys.
- And to every other internal organ in your body.

Take your time to really appreciate your inner organs and thank them for working to their optimum levels for you.

Now come back out of that altered state and feel the wonderful feelings you just projected to yourself. If you do this simple exercise regularly don't be surprised at the results.

Goals

Setting goals is of paramount importance for your future success in all the areas of your life, so it's a good idea to define your goals early on so you know exactly where you're going and how long it's going to take you to get there.

As mentioned previously when you have defined your goals you need to make a map or route to get to where you're going and then take the actions needed to transport you to your desired destination. And if you do it with a determination and passion you will reach it soon enough.

You'll know when you're getting closer to your dream life or goals because you'll feel it and see it in your soul, everything will fall into place and things will keep moving at rapid speed towards your dreams. The closer you get, the more impatient you may get but don't let this little thing get in your way and cloud your judgment, stay on track and keep going - the end result is in sight.

Live your life now in this moment, as this wonderful life is yours already - it's not in the future, it is now. All you are waiting for is to take hold of the possessions that go with the lifestyle.

And lastly it's no use without belief. Belief is the most important part of all of this process, you must believe in your heart and soul that you are already living the life of your dreams and that you deserve it. If it's a new love you're looking for, then seeing the man or women in your mind and continually associating yourself with them as if they are already yours is a similar recipe for success.

Example

Relax and take some deep breaths. Visualise yourself who you want to be, with an image of whom you want to be with. Associate fully into the images as if it were happening already, see how you act with one another, what you say to one another, notice the clothes you're wearing and your hair and skin etc... When you feel totally associated into the images in your mind press the third finger of your left hand together with your thumb and anchor that feeling.

If you did it right whenever you press the thumb and finger together again - you should feel an intense feeling of love and happiness with that person. Keep going through this technique each day until it manifests itself into a reality.

Remember to have faith!

Illness

One of the key factors in getting better from any illness is to have an unwavering faith that things will get better, no matter how bad things are. Your likelihood of getting better goes up by a staggering 50 percent whenever you utilize the part of your brain to generate good feelings and to visualise yourself healthy and happy in the future. It's easy to slip back into feelings of despair and depression when you're ill but you must change your way of thinking to get yourself back to optimum health.

Example

Sit or lie in a quiet room and take some deep breaths. Tell your legs, arms, hands and feet to relax. As your body begins to relax start counting from 100 down to zero, it doesn't matter if you get lost along the way, just allow your mind to drift wherever it wants to go. As images and thoughts begin to drift in and out of your mind start to guide your thoughts now to a time in the near future when you will look and feel completely healthy and happy. If you lose your place just keep bringing the image back and make it bigger and brighter.

As you go through this image in your mind really notice yourself looking healthy and happy. Notice how your body is strong and healthy and how your hair shines and your skin radiates with health and wellbeing. Now I want you to make a small image of the sick you and make it full size right in front of you. Now make a little pocket size image of the healthy happier you we just had.

Next I want you to bring the small healthy happy image of you closer up as the sick big picture starts to shrink out of focus and, as they cross one another, make the switch as quickly as you can. Now do the whole process again and keep doing it at least 5 times until when you think about the sick you and you can no longer get the image in your head, all that's left is the big beautiful image of a radiant healthy happy you.

It's not important to understand how these techniques work and you don't even have to believe them, just have belief in yourself. Do them as often as you can and then relax and see how much more quickly you can regain your health.

Secret Healing System

You have all heard the saying "prevention is better than cure" well this quote just so happens to be true. True health and happiness comes when you pay attention and take appropriate action towards your physical and mental health. Instead of waiting until you get sick to call upon the body's secret healing system, try to start today for there is no other greater time to start your journey to health and happiness. When you're feeling healthy you can't be unhappy, it's a wonderful feeling that nearly everyone has experienced at some time in their life.

Without your health you have nothing, so working on this area of your life first will make it so much easier to succeed in all other areas of your life. Think about it? The best time to check if the parachutes are working is before the plane takes flight, not when it runs into trouble 25 thousand feet above ground.

When you take good care of your health it takes care of you into old age and you get to enjoy all the wonderful things life has to offer. When we can learn how to strengthen the body's healing system without any sign of illness it gives you the positivity to defeat any illness.

Example

An athlete running for a gold medal wouldn't just turn up on the day and expect to win would they? Many hours of physical and mental training are endured before the race so that they can build up the correct muscles in preparation for the day. It's equally important for him to build not just physical power and strength but mental power and strength.

Tap into your own body's natural healing system and notice the outstanding results. I know many people including myself who do not pay daily or weekly visits to the doctor's surgery with their health problems. Instead they have learned how to tap into their own natural healing system. It's not irresponsible to stop putting a burden on your doctor's time if you're feeling unwell, it's about taking more time to claim responsibility for your own health and wellbeing.

It's about developing a clear confidence in your own body and knowing how to cope with the physical challenges in our lives should we need to. These people know how to activate their own healing system by continuously listening to their bodies. You have a built-in healing system that is continuously trying to communicate with you 24 hours a day, so why leave your health in someone else's hands?

I'm not saying you should never visit your doctor, of course that would be absurd, what I'm saying is you can minimize the time you place on your doctor by simply listening to the messages your body is sending off at any one time.

When you do this you can activate the healing system and let the body repair itself naturally without intervention. Your body is a miraculous machine that, believe it or not, can heal and repair itself when you are sick.

You can become your own doctor and prevent illness and disease when you learn these simple techniques. Take control today of your own destiny – here is a prescription for taking control of your healing system.

Prescription for Strengthening Your Healing System

The following techniques are aimed primarily at strengthening your healing system. Whether you're learning for prevention or healing a current illness by paying close attention, you will be able to effectively tap into your body's natural healing system and significantly improve your health.

As already mentioned, your body is always trying to communicate with you on both a conscious and unconscious level. It constantly sends out valuable information to help you know what it needs.

Example

When you're hungry your body tells you by subtly sending messages of hunger such as pains in the tummy or an ache or feeling sick. If you ignore the message it gets louder, and if you continue to ignore it, the body will keep on trying to deliver its message - once you feed it, the body has done its job and won't send another message until the next time you are hungry.

If you are tired the body will feel weak or the eyes feel heavy until you fall into a peaceful sleep. Similarly, when you feel too hot or too cold the messages are always delivered. Just as all these simple messages your body is always sending you, it sends other more subtle messages about your health. For instance if you feel upset for any length of time you may be one of those people who feel a tightness in your chest or your heart missing a beat or two, if you ignore these signals or messages it could lead to more pain or other disastrous consequences.

Even though some of us like to think we listen to our bodies, sometimes it's easy to miss the messages or ignore them hoping they will go away, unless the situation is resolved. Sadly it doesn't go away, it just gets worse and in most cases goes on to cause disastrous results.

If the messages are continually ignored the body will react by alerting you the only way it knows how – usually through intense pain. Therefore to avoid pain and stay healthy we need to become better listeners.

Learning to listen to these early warning signs will avoid illness and disease and your body will no longer need to shout at you!

Listen Up!

In the following techniques you will gain access to important messages from your body's healing system:

- Find a quiet room where you can relax completely.
- Either lie or sit in a comfortable position with or without quiet, relaxing

music playing in the background.

- Take some deep breaths and tell your body to relax.
- Now pay attention to your breathing, as your breaths become slow and gentle.
- Allow your mind to wander away to wherever it chooses still in the quietness of your own body.
- Focus now on the inside of your body like an internal scan machine and notice any internal messages around the brain, heart, liver or kidneys and continue the search slowly stopping at each area and just listening for any messages that might be there.
- After about 10 minutes of this you will feel totally in contact with your body and soul and be able to pick up the subtle messages
- After you have completed the whole scan, send love to each organ in your body with the promise to look after it and care for it through proper nutrition and exercise.

Eventually these techniques will just happen as they become hardwired to your unconscious mind every day. You will begin to enjoy the most exquisite pleasure in your own body as you become more attuned to its sensitivities. Listening to your body is one of the easiest ways to retain health and happiness through the course of your life.

Controlling Your Life

Taking full control of your life isn't just about deciding what dress to wear or which shoes to buy – it's about choosing proper nutrition for your long term health. It's about decisions you make in your personal and professional life. It's about forming lasting, healthy relationships with the people you love and want to be around and most importantly to take full responsibility when things go wrong. It's not someone else's fault when things go wrong in our lives, it's our own. As adults we have the ultimate power to make decisions.

When you feel in control of your life, things can only get better. I've known people come to me for therapy and say "but I can't do that, he wouldn't like it" I say well that's his problem! How can one be happy in any relationship based on what only one person wants or feels about a situation or decision? If you're going to have a healthy, happy relationship it's about two people who care enough about each other to have their say and stand up and be counted.

If you're in a relationship and one person falls out of love with you, or you with them, and you make it difficult for them to leave because of your own pain, then you can be sure it will never last the course anyway. The more difficult it becomes for the person who wants to leave, the more resentment and anger will set in, eventually causing more misery and pain.

No-one said it was easy, matters of the heart never really are. Most of us fall in and out of love throughout our lives many times. I remember a man telling me once after the breakdown of his marriage how he had wasted thirty years with the wrong person.

"Wow," I said, "how on earth did you manage to stay with someone you wasted thirty years with?"

He looked at me and thought for a moment then said "I don't know what you mean".

I said "Well, if you've been with this person for thirty years and been unhappy for thirty years you deserve a medal".

He replied, "No I haven't been unhappy for the whole thirty years," it slowly began to register somewhere in his mind that he had spent many happy years with this person but because she no longer loved him and wanted out of the relationship he thought it had been a complete waste of time.

You see I think if I spent thirty years with someone and then the relationship ended I would expect to feel the pain of losing them so unexpectedly. At the same time I would be thankful for that part of my life with them and know that no matter how long it takes, I would one day look back and know it was for the best taking all the good memories of our time together and leaving the unhappy ones behind.

Hanging on to bad or unpleasant memories can only bring misery and pain and our own unhelpful past programming keeps us from having freedom and making better choices. If you find that you can't make a decision about something important in your life for fear of your partner's reaction then you have to question your own current beliefs about yourself and others.

Changing Your Unconscious Mind

What most of us don't realise is that most of our lives are unconscious. When I was first told this by my tutor, I reacted as many of my own clients did after that and thought he meant my life was predetermined and that the most I could possibly hope for was for me to become more aware of the unconscious programming that was firmly planted in my head.

I later learned from Dr Richard Bandler that that is not necessarily true. Everything you do today affects our conscious and unconscious mind. If I learn something that I believe to be fact then my unconscious mind has been affected or changed but just as our unconscious minds are filled with all the beliefs and values from our parents and other people from birth, we in effect can change some of it, if not all.

It's like growing up with a set of instructions sent to the brain from other bigger, more advanced computers (our parents) and never updating it as we get to adulthood. I'm not saying that all of these beliefs or values will be bad. What I'm saying is how can you function in your own wisdom to the maximum without ever questioning your current belief system to see if it fits?

You may choose to keep some of the old programs or delete a few of them. You may want to get rid of all the old programs and update your full operating software. Either way you will benefit massively from this decision to develop your own mind power. When you first start to question your beliefs you may find it overwhelming in that it doesn't seem real to you. That's because your current beliefs don't actually belong to you, they belong to your parents. It's not that it's even your parents' fault. Parents usually want the best for their children and so they go about teaching them all they know to date without ever questioning the beliefs that came from the same place (their parents) and so the chain goes on repeating itself.

By updating your current software (your brain) you get to make better choices and have a happier life including all we have talked about in this book: health, happiness, prosperity, and most of all freedom. When you start really living your life to its full potential and wake up with a swing in your step you will know how good life can be.

How Can I Re-Program My Mind?

Simple - see a hypnotherapist or follow the full instructions in the next chapter to start updating your mind and start living a fuller life.

Find a quiet place where you can relax in bed or sit in a chair. If you want to play relaxing music now would be a good time to put it on and darken the room slightly.

As you begin to take some deep breaths feel your body relax, instruct your mind to do so by simple commands such as relaxing the muscles around the eyes. As you go on, relax the muscles in the arms, legs and back. Keep taking deep breaths for about 60 seconds then start counting from 100 down to zero.

As you count, feel the muscles in your body starting to relax even more. Now I want you to pay attention to your breathing as it slows down to a quiet, peaceful rhythm. You may find that you begin to drift in and out of this altered state of awareness but don't worry it's perfectly normal.

As you keep drifting allow your mind to just drift as different thoughts pop in and out - don't try to stop them, just go with the flow. Now when you're sufficiently relaxed ask your mind to bring up the past experience or belief you no longer wish to have and make it big full size in colour. Now I want you to get an image of the new belief or experience you wish to have in a small box like a matchbox size and place it in the left hand corner of the bigger image you no longer want.

As the big image gets smaller, drifting out of focus, the smaller new image you want to have gets bigger. Now as they cross each other I want you to make a switch as quickly as you can so that all that's left is the new image you want to have fully in front of you and the old outdated ones gone.

Open and close your eyes a few times and now see if you can get the old images back, no matter how hard it may be, try and I bet it's gone for good, or at least very difficult for you to recall it. It's amazing what you can do with your mind.

People – you don't have to suffer, you can use your brain for change!

27

Using Your Own Energy

All living things are energy. Or have a magnetic energy field surrounding them, that magnetic energy field is interconnected to universal energy. As human beings are living things we have this energetic field that guides us through our lives, we are just not aware of it.

But what if you could be? You are more powerful than your every day mind can imagine, in fact your thoughts are energy and thoughts control your feelings. Everything you think about has an impact on your feelings and your feelings have an impact on your every day experiences. Think about that for a moment? If your thoughts control your feelings isn't it a good idea to make them good ones?

We also have energy centres that are affected by our thinking. Another way of putting it is; what you continually think about most ie: money, sex, love, career, confidence, or lack of it, you get more of.

Those energy centres are referred to as chakras. In eastern traditions the chakras in the ancient language of Sanskrit means wheel. The body has many of these wheels or chakras but most healers will only deal with the major ones. Most chakras can be located next to a hormonal gland in the body and push outwards vital life force energy also known as" Chi" or" Ki "or "Prana" by the ancient yogis.

Using the chakras to heal ourselves puts us in touch with our psychic abilities. Mostly our psychic abilities are left undetected. In the modern world people have closed off the psychic part of their brain that was used daily by our ancestors - back then we used more of our psychic abilities to make sense of the world. Just like a farmer knows when it will rain by reading the skies and his animals or new born babies use their five senses because they have nothing else to make sense of the world they now live in. Notice how your baby will cry when it's hungry or to alert you it's in pain.

As we get older we start to use more of our conscious abilities and continue learning through parents, friends and family until we almost lose touch with ourselves and lock our natural psychic abilities away, not trusting ourselves to be accurate anymore.

Have you ever had a feeling the phone was going to ring and it did, or thought about someone you know or haven't seen for ages and all of a sudden you bump into them? That's your own natural psyche sending messages to your brain. Our bodies are always sending off messages to use but we tend to ignore them most of the time. I call this the 21st century disease that needs to be updated.

When you have negative thoughts, your chakras (energy centres) become blocked or grey and can't get enough vital

213

force energy through so you may become depressed or feel down, a bit like you might on a grey winter's day.

You have many chakras that are responsible for each of your thoughts such as money, love, relationships or career. If your thoughts about these things are good, then your chakras will work in perfect harmony and you will experience feelings of joy and love. However if your thoughts about them are bad, then you will have feelings of despair and fear.

Your natural state is one of intuitive creative energy, if you're not feeling this way or, worse still, have never felt this way, then you clearly have some work to do on your chakras but once you have cleansed all your chakras you will be uplifted and full of this wonderful intuitive energy that is rightfully yours from birth.

Cleansing Your Chakras (Energy Centres)

Root Chakra
Location: Bottom of Spine.
Colour: Red
Spins Slow

Because the root chakra spins slower than the other major chakras it sends off a brilliant ruby-red colour. When this root chakra is clean it will usually have sparkling white lights, intermingled with the vibrant red. However if the chakra gets blocked or dirty it will become dull in colour.

Your root chakra is affected by thoughts and feelings about:

- Money - bills, gambling, retirement, economy.
- Career - having enough money, your job.
- Home - feeling safe, buying a home.
- Needs - having enough of something like clothes, love.
- Possessions - cars, jewellery.

Any fears related to any of the above will shrink or block your root chakra or it will become dirty. If your feelings are of poor quality (never enough to go round) this will act as a self-fulfilling prophecy.

Sacral Chakra
Location: Between naval and bottom of spine.
Colour: Orange
Spins a little faster than root chakra

When the sacral chakra is balanced it will appear a beautiful shade of orange with a clear brilliant white interior, if this chakra is dirty or unbalanced it will be of a burnt orange colour.

Your sacral chakra is affected by thoughts and feelings to do with:

- Cravings - food, drink, sex and other thrill seeking activities.
- Addictions - drugs, alcohol or food.
- Habits - sleep, weight gain or loss, self-image.

If you are worried about any of the above or feeling down or have no confidence in these areas your chakra will appear to be shrunken or dirty or both resulting in you experiencing feelings of forgetfulness and tiredness.

Heart Chakra
Location: Centre of Chest
Colour: Green
Spins: Medium Fast Speed

The heart chakra is the beginning of the upper chakras which correspond to spiritual issues, unlike the lower chakras which correspond to physical and material issues. This chakra, which is a most beautiful green colour, spins at a medium fast speed. When this chakra is clean and working perfectly it is an Luminescent emerald green.

The Heart chakra is affected by thoughts and feelings to do with:

- Relationships - mothers, fathers, children, spouses, friends and siblings.
- Attachments - obsessions about people, addictions.
- Learning to forgive oneself and others.

- Clear future vision - understanding, guidance, etc

Any fears you may have about love or the lack of it will affect the heart chakra and it will become enlarged and clogged - this will stop you from experiencing deeper love and understanding of oneself and others. Unfortunately most of us have experienced love pain and so we automatically associate pain with love, this is not a good way to associate love, try now to disassociate your love for someone or something with pleasure instead of pain.

Long term blockage means long term pain in your heart that eventually spreads to other parts of the body, so you will experience pain elsewhere.

Throat Chakra
Location: Adams apple.
Colour: Sky Blue
Spins at a fast rate.

A clean throat chakra spins at a fast rate and looks similar to what you would see on a clear bright sunny day. If it is dirty it will look like a grey, misty day.

The throat chakra is affected by:

- Truthfulness towards yourself and others, clients, customers, audiences and people you know.
- Writing, horse riding ,singing, dancing, artistic tendencies, teaching.
- Asking for what you want for yourself and others etc

When you have fears of communicating effectively with yourself and other's the list above the throat chakra will shrink and often cause physical discomfort or even pain in the throat area.

Ear Chakra
Location: Inside your head just above either ear
Colour: Violet /Red
Spins quickly.

The ear chakra rests just above your left and right ears inside your head and sits at a 30 degree angle. The ear chakra sends off beautiful rays of violet and red and when the ear chakra is clean it should look clear and sharp mingled with flashes of white and purple. Dirty ear chakras have no light coming through and will appear opaque and muddy.

The ear chakra is affected by:

- Spirituality.
- Communicating with your higher self.
- Mentally re-playing things you have heard yourself or someone else say.
- Unforgivingness towards yourself and others.
- Spiritual messages.
- Divine beings.

Third Eye Chakra
Location: Between the eyes
Colour: Indigo Blue

The third eye chakra is also known as 'The Eye of Shiva' in many eastern traditions. If you were to close your eyes now and take a few deep breaths and look between your eyes on the inside you would begin to see or feel an oval shaped object lying sideways. This is a natural phenomena and it is your third eye. Sometimes it can appear closed or half open or even flicker open and closed. It is usually looking right at you. There is no need to fear this third eye looking at you it is your true self or higher self and is there to protect you throughout your life.

There is a good reason that your third eye is laid on its side and is looking towards you is that everything is inside (within you) nothing else except what is in your heart and mind. Your life as you know it is an illusion. It is an Illusion that a separate world exists outside of you and separate from you. Your third eye records movies about your life inside your head throughout your entire life, it will include everything you feel, think, and do. It also will record every emotion felt by other people who have had contact with you in this life. After you pass over to the other side it is said you watch this movie before you die.

The third eye chakra is affected by:

- Your future, the past, your psychic abilities, clairvoyance, etc
- Beliefs about things you cannot see, feel or hear.

When the third eye chakra is clean you will see your higher self (third eye) looking at you. If the third eye is closed it will block out all your spiritual vision and intuition.

Crown Chakra
Location: Inside the top of your head
Colour: Vivid Royal Blue
Spins Fast.

Imagine the crown chakra as if you were looking at a ceiling fan that is coloured in a vivid royal blue. We receive information vital to our life force energy through the crown chakra continually receiving information and ideas we can tap into a wealth of creativity available through the crown chakra.

The crown chakra is affected by:

- Universal laws and creation and our beliefs about it.
- Spirituality, negative experiences with religion, un-forgiveness towards people.
- Divine intervention, receiving messages from the divine source of energy.
- The aesthetic plane, medium-ship, knowing, trust.

A clean crown chakra will send a beautiful shade of royal blue /purple with speckles of white light. Clogged crown chakras will leave you feeling bitter and lonely.

Fortunately all our major chakras respond to cleansing techniques and you can start your own cleansing journey now. Cleansing your chakras daily or weekly will ensure you stay in that all natural state of awareness.

Clean up your act

As human beings we are constantly being bombarded with information on a daily basis, unfortunately we don't always get to choose if this information is true or even good for us. All our decisions are nearly unconscious and even if they are conscious they soon become unconscious. We are constantly told that being a size 12 is too big and we need to get slimmer or we are useless. This affects are thoughts and our feelings about how we should and shouldn't behave.

Clearing negative beliefs about yourself will greatly improve your health and wellbeing more than you can imagine and if you use these techniques along with other mind programming techniques taught in this book you will feel much happier, healthier and become more successful in everything you do.

Relax it's easy

All the best things come from relaxation so when you learn to relax more often you get to have better quality thoughts and feelings that can and will change your life forever. Look at this grid below to get used to the colours before you start your meditation.

Crown Chakra(Sahastrara)

Third Eye(Ajna)

Throat(Vishudda)

Heart Plexux(Anahata)

Solar Plexus(Manipur)

Sacral or Spleenic(Hara)

Root(Muladhara)

Once you can visualise the colour relating to the chakra or (Energy Centre) you can begin your meditation.

If you're new to meditation relax, don't worry it will come naturally, you are no different to anyone else, we all have that divine power we were born with.

First find somewhere you can relax and be alone where no-one can disturb you. This might be in your bedroom, living room or garden - indeed anywhere just so long as you can't be disturbed for the next thirty minutes.

Sitting comfortably or lying down is preferable to standing but if you need to stand don't worry it will have the same affect, your body knows its own wisdom. Make sure the room is warm so you don't become too cold when sitting for any length of time.

Now close your eyes and take some really deep breaths in through your nose and out through your mouth. You will begin to notice your body relaxing, ask your head to relax then your neck and shoulders, now ask yourself to relax your arms and legs feeling the muscles relaxing further. Ask your chest and back muscles to relax and feel your muscles relaxing even more. Again ask yourself to relax the muscles in your arms and legs feeling the muscles relaxing more and more as you experience a sweet soft gentle feeling of letting go.

As you relax, your ego may try to distract you from relaxing. It actually does this because it's afraid you won't come back once you have found peace in your mind – it thinks you might not need it anymore.

If you become peaceful and calm, your ego loses all its power as the old programmes collapse. Don't worry, just allow all the thoughts and feelings your ego sends your way to float in and out without trying to fight it. It will eventually stop as you become more aware and focused in peace and tranquillity. If you have any fears at all, you should see them and then let them go. You can do this by imagining the fear as a bubble and then watching as the bubble bursts and disappears out of sight and mind as if it were an illusion. As you watch it burst and disappear you can breathe in peace and love.

Affirmations in meditation are an important part of letting go of old habits and cleansing your body and soul. You should use them often for maximum affect.

As you continue in the relaxed state say to yourself 'I am willing to let go of old habits and beliefs about myself and others'. I can see clearly now and visualise a cleansing, brilliant white light flooding through your crown chakra down through each of your other major chakras stopping at each one to be cleansed. Visualise each chakra as this divine white light travels through your body asking for everything your heart desires. See and feel each one of your chakras completely cleansed and illuminating its brilliant colour.

Stay in this state of hypnosis for a while, don't rush it, until you can feel the universal energy inside you. Sometimes people say they feel like crying after this cleansing as if something miraculous has just happened.

It's your body's way of releasing the old self so let the tears flow, you will feel absolutely exhilarated afterwards.

Remember to smile at yourself when it's done!

28

Trees And Healing Energy

Trees have an apparent ecological health benefit that is apparent in today's world. Some people like me believe trees to be symbols of life and guardians of ecology. Their roots actually anchor in the soil and prevent landslides. Their leaves and branches act as a shield to protect the temperature of the rivers where the fish swim. Through photosynthesis, trees capture the carbon-dioxide from the air and nutrients from the earth and energy from the sun to produce oxygen.

Studies have shown that poplar trees have the ability to remove dangerous chemicals from the soil. The harmful chemicals are released through the leaves. Tree energy is used by the ancient Celts to promote healing in our toxic bodies.

Trees have one of the longest life spans known to man, and are a powerful natural symbol of stability and longevity throughout the world. They, along with other plants, minerals, and the earth itself emit unique energy vibrations. These vibrations of energy can be channelled through our own bodies and help to rid the body of toxic energy, without doing any harm to the tree.

Trees ultimately enrich our lives with their energy and presence. For without them we could not live.

To clear yourself of negativity find a tree that you are particularly drawn to and ask permission to give it the negative energy that you have unknowingly stored in your body. Trees don't mind if you give it to them as they can use it to their own enhancement.

To release stored up negative emotional and physical energy and bring the trees life force energy deep inside you, simply run your left hand from the top of your head down your right side of your body to the bottom of your feet visualising a colour you associate with negative energy and imagine your hand collecting it as you sweep your hands all the way down.

Now do the same with your right hand, run it down the left side of your body from the head to toes, again visualising the collection of your coloured negative energy leaving your body. Don't underestimate the power of thought. Do this about three to five times and then sit under the tree with your spine directly up against the trunk. You will begin to notice a tingling sensation throughout your body as you imagine a bright luminous light travelling from the top of the tree down into the crown of your head. Fill yourself up with the universal life force energy.

Before you go, thank the tree for allowing you to give it the negative energy.

29

Learning Should Be Fun

There should be a law that states learning should be fun. That way people would learn quicker and easier and most importantly have fun doing so. When kids learn at school, it should be compulsory that it's fun for them. When kids are having fun they learn much quicker. The trouble with that is we have a whole learning system that can't even teach itself.

Teachers, I've found, are the most pessimistic of all next to doctors and medical people whose learning are outdated and worse, still don't work. People often confuse laughter and fun with not learning as if it's something we should be ashamed of. They think if you're having too much fun then you can't be learning. Bullshit! I say, sorry about the French but it's something which I'm passionate about. You see I grew up with these kind of teachers and I didn't learn anything. In fact we were punished for smiling. Can you imagine that – punished because you looked like you were having a good time or you looked too happy?

I was raised in a strict catholic family and I was sent to a catholic high school for girls where you couldn't even speak without permission. How can that kind of behaviour teach you anything other than how to hate yourself and not relate to people?

Even by today's standards it isn't much better. Ok, kids aren't allowed to be smacked anymore but teachers still have these outdated views. I read a report recently about teachers deliberately mislabelling kids as having learning difficulties or being dyslexic to cover up their own poor teaching skills and worst of all, to get more resources for the school. It is reported that 1.7 million kids are down as having learning difficulties in England but the report says only half of those need better learning and are no different to other kids.

How's that for a slap in the face considering the fact most kids usually believe what they're told at such a young tender age? I believe such teachers should be banned from teaching, after all you wouldn't trust someone with your life who didn't know how to help you?

I was one of those kids who grew up believing I didn't have a chance in life and I was thick because the school said I was, so they must be right? WRONG! I wasn't any different to most kids in my school that could learn. In fact, I have probably learnt more than most kids in my school in my lifetime up to present. These people who are responsible for your education and welfare inside schools should start learning themselves, there are very few teachers who are good anymore and do it because they love it.

I know of many more highly qualified skilled people in various professions that have had similar experiences as me and

I'm sure there are many more, it is a shame for those young, vulnerable children because only a small percent actually learn as they get older that they can do anything they want like I did, most will just accept what has been confirmed to them from teachers and then their un-knowing parents. Unfortunately for these kids it doesn't stop there, it causes untold damage to their confidence, self esteem and job prospects.

Laughter and happiness open up your ability to learn. How many of you get serious when you're learning something? With the belief that if you're having fun you can't learn? Learning to open yourself up to laughter and having fun isn't so hard to do and you spread that happiness and laughter to others. Notice how time flies when you're having fun and how time goes on forever when you stand in line. I've known teachers who have walked about for weeks and months without smiling once. How on earth do they do that? To me they've been teaching too long and not learning enough.

How can anyone who doesn't learn anything be qualified to teach you? That's always baffled me; it's just yet another example of how our world is falling apart with people in high placed professions who have no idea of their own actions to others. I know I go on a bit but I'm passionate about people and learning, it's something that completely took me by surprise to find there are people walking this planet who have no desire to learn new things. You may say I am naive. Yes, I admit that but I'm passionate and I strive every day of my life to learn and know more about the world we live in. Could it be because I was deprived of an education? Possibly.

I'm a great believer in people and I believe when people

have the facts they will take appropriate action. People are smarter and want more from life and so they should, you don't have to feel bad anymore at wanting success – take it, it's yours to have.

And remember learning is power and power is control, and there's nothing like having control of your own brain, so why not start a journey of self-discovery and see how much more you can learn? Happiness doesn't just belong to the chosen few it belongs to you too.

Happiness comes from within, you don't have to look outside yourself to attain it. People often complicate life – yet life isn't complicated, it's simple keep things simple and life will present many opportunities.

Your journey is just as important as anyone else's. You only need to adjust yourself to your environment and watch as your dreams unfold.

And remember:

Think of This If You should Ever Feel Not Good Enough?

"I have nothing to Declare except My Genius"

OSCAR WILDE

Contact Helen direct:

Telephone 07702792668

Email: nell10_@hotmail.com

www.tohealyourlife.webs.com

Keep a look out for Helen's next book 'Genius Kids'

Children respond well to hypnosis and parents should learn simple techniques to help their children when in difficult situations. This is covered in Helen's book 'Genius Kids' and dispels the myths of hypnosis to give you a clearer understanding of how it can be applied in your child's life.

"Children have always believed in magic," says Helen, "all I do is help them to through guided imagery with the Magic Carpet Technique , and it works brilliantly every time."

All child consultations to the above email address .

Best wishes,
Helen